CALL
OF THE
NORTH
WIND

VOYAGES AND
ADVENTURES
ON LAKE SUPERIOR

BY MARLIN BREE

MARLOR PRESS, INC.

Saint Paul, Minnesota

CALL
OF THE
NORTH
WIND

Illustrations by Marlin Bree

Mary Strasma, Assistant Editor
Cover design by Maclean & Tuminelly

Distributed in the U.S.A. to the book trade
by Contemporary Books, Inc.,
Chicago, Illinois

ISBN 943400-90-2

Portions of Chapter Three have previously appeared in *SAILING* Magazine.
Chapter Six has appeared in *NORTHERN BREEZES* Magazine.

Manufactured in the United States of America

First edition

MARLOR PRESS, INC.
4304 Brigadoon Drive
Saint Paul, Minnesota 55126

CONTENTS

STORM CROSSING

FOR

THOSE WHO LOVE BIG WATERS

AND ESPECIALLY FOR

LORIS & WILL

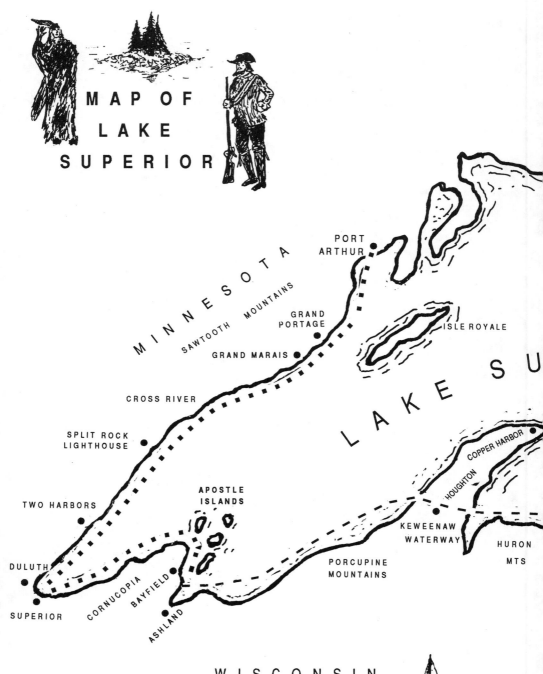

MAP OF LAKE SUPERIOR

MINNESOTA

PORT ARTHUR

SAWTOOTH MOUNTAINS

GRAND PORTAGE

ISLE ROYALE

GRAND MARAIS

CROSS RIVER

LAKE SU

SPLIT ROCK LIGHTHOUSE

COPPER HARBOR

HOUGHTON

TWO HARBORS

APOSTLE ISLANDS

KEWEENAW WATERWAY

HURON MTS

DULUTH

PORCUPINE MOUNTAINS

CORNUCOPIA

BAYFIELD

SUPERIOR

ASHLAND

WISCONSIN

VOYAGE OF *PERSISTENCE* ▪ ▪ ▪ ▪

VOYAGE OF *TULLAMORE DEW* ▬ ▬ ▬

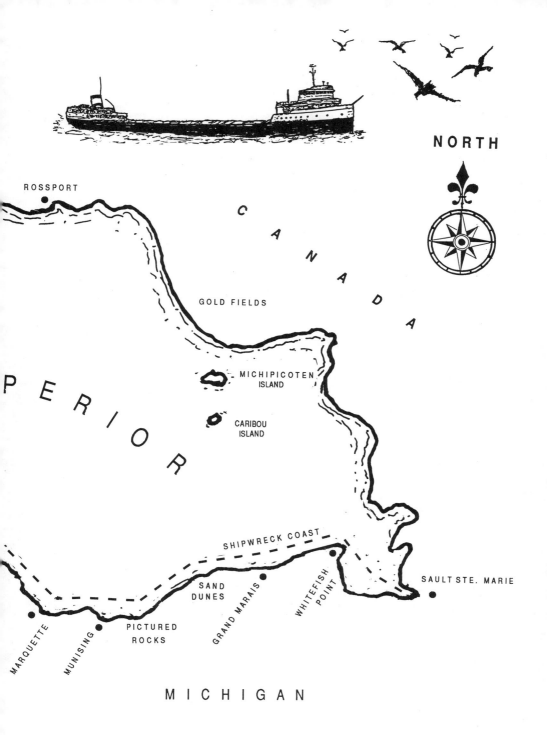

ROSSPORT

C A N A D A

GOLD FIELDS

NORTH

P E R I O R

MICHIPICOTEN
ISLAND

CARIBOU
ISLAND

SHIPWRECK COAST

SAULT STE. MARIE

SAND
DUNES

GRAND MARAIS

WHITEFISH
POINT

PICTURED
ROCKS

MARQUETTE

MUNISING

M I C H I G A N

LAKE SUPERIOR: ● Covers 31,280 square miles, the largest lake in the world
by surface area ● Contains ten percent of the world's fresh surface water —
three quadrillion (3,000,000,000,000,000) gallons, enough to cover all of
Canada, the United States, Mexico, and South America with one foot of water.

BAPTISM
BY THE
THREE SISTERS

THE STORM RAGED FOR DAYS, then seemed to blow itself out. What was left over were the sloppy rollers from the northeast that charged heavily toward the shore.

Of course, northeast was the direction I wanted to sail.

It seemed once again that Lake Superior was not cooperating with me. Not that it ever did, but on this particular morning, I was convinced that I could do something by sheer dint of nerve about the storms that left me on a lee shore.

I was getting a little anxious. As fall approached, I was behind schedule. I had been warned that I could sail Superior's north shore from mid-July to mid-August, but after that the lake couldn't be trusted. It was nearly September.

I had been in my small sailboat all that summer of 1984 since embarking on the Fourth of July from Bayfield, Wisconsin. Originally, I had intended to sail as much as the world's largest freshwater sea as I could — maybe even to circumnavigate its 2,900 miles of shoreline. But as I sailed the beautiful Apostle Islands, cruised the western shore of Wisconsin down to Duluth and Superior, and, finally, made my way by water up the North Shore, I had become fascinated with what I found and heard about the Big Lake. I sailed more and more slowly.

Each night, I would pull out a tattered copy of *Lake Superior* by Grace Lee Nute, published in 1944. By the light of a portable lantern, snuggled in my sleeping bag, I read the book's descriptions of some of the routes and sights of the voyageurs and early sailors. The next day, I sailed what I had read about. Along the way, I talked with waterfront people, who told me stories about shipwrecks, colorful history, sea captains, local characters, and fierce storms.

However, as I sailed out of the harbor of refuge where I had spent another anxious night, I began to regret my delays. My 20-foot-long, home-built centerboard sailboat bucked through the waves, and just to remind me where I was, the bow dug in a bit, then flung spray backwards. I caught some in my face. I always hated that, because the spray not only made it difficult for me to see but reminded me how close and cold the lake was.

My glasses began to fog up from the inside, and I recalled one of the local tales I had collected on my voyage: that of the Three Sisters. That was the name the French voyageurs gave to the phenomenon of three waves in a row, each wave bigger than the first. These sisters were much feared by the voyageurs, whose thousand mile-paddle out of New Canada culminated in crossing this fiercest of lakes.

I tugged once again to check my safety harness, which was secured to the cabin by stainless steel bolts; it gave me a little comfort. I was alone in the small cockpit, feeling the nearness of the water around me. The boat's heavy wooden cabin hatch was sealed shut, a security precaution in case a wave came onboard. That was possible, for *Persistence* sat just a few feet above the waterline.

Suddenly, a howl came out of nowhere: the storm had returned. The boat heeled under the onslaught, then righted herself. It was amazing how quickly the waves could build. The wind seemed to scoop water into troughs, then push them up, higher and higher, to form the speeding square rollers that Superior is famous for.

The boat was being overpowered by the wind and waves. Quickly, I dropped my sails and swung down the five-horsepower outboard. I yanked yard on the starter; with a roar, the engine came to life.

Engine snarling, we tore defiantly toward a large wave. With a "whump" noise, the bow slammed into the moving water, spray flying. The momentum carried us past the crest, but the bow tipped up, making me feel like I was on a teeter-totter. After a moment of balancing on the wave's top, the bow pointed downward into the trough.

Immediately, the engine began to race dangerously. The outboard's propeller had come out of the water, along with much of the rudder. We teetered out of control, then a fraction of a second later, the bow slid down the side of the wave; the engine dug in with a powerful roar as the propeller dipped back in the water.

We were moving now, heading toward the second wave. I wondered what would happen next.

I didn't have long to look at the wall of water moving at me. We were still heading down when the bow dug in again, this time at the base of the onrushing water. The wave crashed over the bow.

Now it was not just spray everywhere, but solid water we were plunging into. I felt the boat below me lift as the wave crashed down on the bow, pushing it down. The stern where I sat lifted.

I felt a lump of fear in my throat; my eyeglasses fogged over again. In the open cockpit, I grabbed anything I could hold onto. My right hand steered with the tiller as my left arm wrapped around a winch. I moved as far forward as I could go, still clutching the tiller. I wrapped my left leg around the mid-cockpit traveler bar.

The bow was being pushed down, and water rolled back toward me in a solid mass. I could smell the water, so close. It buried the bow completely, swirling up and around the cabin. I felt like I was on a submarine.

Just as it seemed as though were going to be pitched stern

over bow, a little miracle happened. The bow lifted, then seemed to shake off the water. We were free again.

There was a lot of noise: Wind shrieked in the rigging; waves sloshed angrily as they charged past us, the lashed sails rattled, and the engine snarled. Above all this racket, I heard yet another noise — it sounded like a waterfall.

I made the mistake of turning my head and immediately wished I hadn't. Another wave train, so large that it simply ran at an angle to the other wave trains and all the way over them, was charging in my direction.

Whump! I felt the bow dig in and the stern rise; we were lifted up and up. I jammed the tiller over to correct our course, but the rushing water seemed to take charge of the boat. We had no steering.

The wave passed; then another one.

Now came the third wave. It loomed over me; we lifted sideways, as if we were on a watery elevator. I felt the wave take hold of my boat's side; the mast canted down toward the onrushing water — we were that far over. I felt the wave's coldness coming toward my face.

We were being levered down. The mast spreader was sticking into the wave. Water sloshed into the cockpit; I recoiled from its icy touch, and I braced myself for the worst.

Just when I thought we couldn't come back, *Persistence* popped up again, waving her mast back and forth, shaking off water. I turned the boat as quickly as I could, so that the next wave caught us on our stern, giving us a shove forward. The larger waves were past, but I was running with them — running for my life.

What seemed like hours later, I passed through the breakwaters of a harbor. A fisherman on the wind-swept pier, secure on his concrete ledge, watched me bowl through the entryway. By the astonished look on his face, I am certain he was wondering what I was doing out here in the first place.

Come to think of it, so was I. I had met three waves in a row, each one bigger than the one before, and survived. Had my little boat and I been baptized by the Three Sisters?

The encounter haunted me. I vowed to return.

PART ONE

ANSWERING
THE
CALL
OF THE
NORTH
WIND

CHAPTER ONE

RETURN
TO SUPERIOR

THE SUN HAD BURNISHED my little boat's wood an amber hue.
Here and there, showing through the rich patina of varnish
were a few dark spots where I had filled the occasional dings,
dents and cuts that came over the years to a little wooden sailboat. After all, *Persistence* was not new.

She was, in fact, almost 17 years old. I had built her by hand
beside my home in Shoreview, Minnesota, and she had survived the ignoble and rough life of a trailerable boat, jounced
over many a bumpy road. Under sail, at anchor, or at a mooring
or a slip, she had weathered a lot of storms.

Her first big adventure came about 12 years ago when I sailed
her on Lake Superior. I began my voyage on the world's largest
freshwater lake (by surface area) at Bayfield, Wisconsin,
cruised throughout the Apostle Islands, then headed down to
the Twin Port cities of Duluth, Minnesota, and Superior, Wisconsin.

As I attempted to sail up Minnesota's spectacular and rugged

North Shore, a northeaster caught me. After repeated bouts on the big lake, I limped into Thunder Bay, Ontario. My little boat had taken a beating in Superior's high waves and winds.

There was no getting around the fact that the boat was becoming aged — and for that matter, so was I.

As I crawled around *Persistence*, first underneath the trailer to check the hull bottom and then inside the cabin to scan the bilge, I reflected on the fact that the boat appeared to have aged well. Her hull and structure were strong and solid. There were no cracks in the wood, no stress marks or crazing or cracking in the epoxy and fiberglass, nor any rot in any major structural area. With just a little epoxy here and there, some new bottom paint and another coat of varnish, she would be ready to sail again.

Slowly I revarnished the wood, and rebuilt one hatch board, where a bottom corner had rotted out. A few cracks in the cabin's coach roof were patched up with epoxy. Underneath, I scraped the hull's bottom and then repainted the green anti-fouling.

I took a final walk around my handiwork as the boat sat securely on its trailer. I had checked the hull, the rigging, the mast — everything had been carefully gone over.

Persistence glowed beautifully in the sunlight. She was ready to go.

And so, more or less, was I.

For some time, I had pondered why I wanted to take my small sailboat out again on Superior. I certainly had my share of troubles in 1984, when I learned that a lightweight, small sailboat didn't have the power to stand up very effectively to Superior's storms. I had felt humbled.

Yet here I was again, ready to try another sailing adventure. Why couldn't I be a normal tourist and just drive around the big lake? Millions of tourists did that. There certainly was enough lake to see — days and days of driving to get around its immense shoreline.

Somehow, it wasn't quite the same to me.

The lake exudes a mystical quality. To really experience the lake, it seems to me, you have to be *on* it. A small sailboat gives you the right perspective. It is a wonderful way to explore a lake. You are close to the water. You appreciate the lake. And you respect the lake. Boy, do you respect the lake.

With less fuss than I expected, my Suzuki Sidekick charged through all five gears and soon we were on the freeway, heading north from our Shoreview home to Lake Superior, the boat on its trailer behind us. My plan was to drive the freeways as much as possible, since they were long and straight, to stay in the right hand lane, and cruise at the minimum legal speed.

I had stuffed everything I needed into the boat's 20-foot length: sleeping bags, food, fuel, water, sails, lines and anchors. Was it my imagination — or did the small trailer tires bulge outward?

"We'll take it easy," I explained to Loris. "We're not trying to set any speed records."

I thought I saw a wifely eyebrow arch. We'd be grinding away at 55 mph, towing a boat behind my sturdy little four-wheeler. We weren't sure how well its small four-cylinder engine would pull the boat and rig in the hills around Superior.

"We'll stop often, to check the rig," I added.

Her expression was not exactly pleased. Still, I reminded myself, she had agreed to help.

About fifty minutes later, I felt something odd in the rig. A vibration.

"You're losing a wheel!" a passing motorist yelled as I exited the freeway toward a rest area.

I felt a cold chill in the pit of my stomach. The left trailer wheel canted at an odd angle. In fact, three of the lug nuts that held the rim to the axle were missing. Just one lug nut was all that was securing the wheel.

I jammed my automobile jack under the trailer axle to take the weight off the wheel, then unhooked the Sidekick and drove to an auto parts store at a nearby small town. With new lug nuts, I carefully tightened on the wheel, this time adding a thread-locking agent. I breathed a sigh of relief as I began driving again, my boat following obediently behind. Problem solved — my voyage was on again!

Or was it? I felt in my back jeans pocket — my wallet was missing! Gone were the funds I had saved for my trip.

We backtracked to the parking area, and I crawled on the concrete below several rigs to see if my wallet had fallen where we had parked. No luck. I checked with the caretaker; no one had turned in a wallet.

"Where did you buy the lug nuts?" Loris asked. I hauled out the receipt. It had a telephone number and Loris made a call. "They've got your wallet!" Loris yelled. Minutes later, I was back at the store, where the manager told me that I had left my wallet on the counter. "We figured you'd be back," he said cheerfully as he handed me my wallet. The money was still there.

"It's a sign," I thought to myself. As we got underway again, the notion crossed my mind that this would be a very different voyage.

How right I was.

The plan was to rendezvous with our friends Ruth and Curtis Johnson at their Good Earth shop near the Cornucopia, Wisconsin, waterfront. Here I would launch *Persistence* and begin my adventure, sailing from Cornucopia, past Sand Island, through the Apostles, then end up at Port Superior, where I would meet Loris. We'd spend some time cruising the Apostles. Later on, I'd cross Superior on a cruising catamaran.

I was optimistic. Sure, we'd had problems with the trailer, but we had solved them. All we had to do was launch *Persistence* to get back on schedule.

I stopped for gas at a small Wisconsin station, topping up the Sidekick's gas tank as well as filling the outboard's gas tank and the boat's spare gas cans. As I drove away from the gas pump, I heard a loud cracking noise — and found that part of my trailer was lying on the ground. It was the right guide-on, a fiberglass pole about an inch in diameter that guided the boat from the water onto the trailer. I had come too close to the gas pumps and a concrete barrier had snapped the pole off. Shaken, and muttering darkly, I tossed the guide-on into the sailboat.

As I started driving again, I reflected that this was turning out to be quite a day. I had obviously encountered my full quota of bad luck.

The law of averages said it had to end here.

We arrived late in the afternoon, greeted the Johnsons, and quickly made preparations to launch the boat at the Cornucopia public launch site. It was small, but so was my boat. I backed the trailer as Loris guided me in. The boat was partly in the water when I felt something bump and I heard a cracking noise — then a splash.

"Your motor is in the water!" Loris yelled.

A sinking feeling came over me. This was the worst luck of all. Without an engine I could not make the journey. I ran into the water and carefully picked up the engine, cradling it in my arms. Water poured from it as I returned to shore.

"The wheel must've hit an underwater hole," I said. "The outboard swung down, jammed in the ramp and snapped off."

It had been over in seconds. Here we were, on a Sunday, on a holiday Fourth of July weekend; there were no outboard repair shops in this area, even assuming the engine could be fixed. I briefly considered going back home to bed, pulling the covers over my head and hibernating for the rest of the boating season.

"Let's see the Johnsons," Loris suggested. Inside the busy Good Earth shop along the waterfront the Johnsons were, as ever, gracious, and moreover, they had an idea. Curtis made a telephone call; a few minutes later, I saw someone dashing down the road on a motorbike. It was Jerry Deering, the marina manager at Cornucopia.

"Heard you had a problem," Jerry said. "Follow me." Minutes later, he introduced me to fellow boater Al Capriglione. Al had two outboard engines on his large fishing boat.

"Can I rent your spare engine?" I asked.

"No," Al said cheerfully, "but you can borrow it." He hoisted his spare Johnson ten-horsepower engine off its transom mount. "It's not new," he explained, "but it ran good the last time I used it." Then he gave me a dented red fuel container. "Use this gas first," he said. "It's two years old."

"You're not giving him the spare kicker off your boat, are you?" his wife interjected.

"We've got our VHF and there are lots of boats out there." Al was not concerned.

I hefted the old Johnson onto my boat. It was a big, heavy engine, and it sank *Persistence's* stern down a couple of inches. When I tried to start it, the engine balked. I kept yanking the starter until I panted from exhaustion.

"We need some young muscles on this," Jerry, who was standing nearby, observed. I saw him motion to a young athlete, who, muscles bulging, whipped the starter twice — and the old outboard chugged to life in a puff of blue smoke.

On the way through the small Cornucopia harbor to our slip in front of the Johnsons' shop, the motor ran wonderfully. My mood lifted. The agreement I had with Al was that I would return his motor as soon as I made it through the Apostles.

Later that day, Ruth Johnson pointed out, "Just think of what *could* have happened." Loris and I were relaxing with the Johnsons's at their Bayfield farmhouse and flower garden. I had been recounting my accidents today — despite my careful preparations.

"Think of all the help you got from wonderful people who stepped forward when you needed them," Curtis added.

I tried to look forward to the rest of the voyage — presuming I could get the outboard started. And provided that the weather, and Superior, cooperated.

After all, I had already had all the bad luck that was to befall me.

Or so I thought.

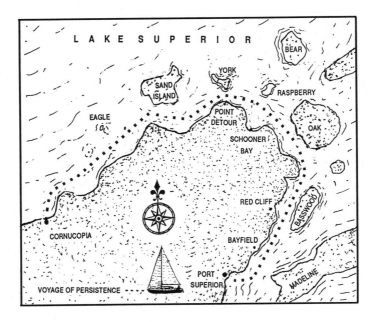

CHAPTER TWO

GREETINGS
OF A
NORTHEASTER

IT WAS A GRAY, WINDY MORNING as I began the first leg of my trip. Ominously, the wind had switched to the northeast — the very direction I was heading — and gusts howled around tiny Cornucopia's waterfront, tugging at my boat's furled sails. Though it was July, I was bundled up in my heavy sweatwear and foul weather gear.

I began preparations to get underway. Would the old engine start? I gave it some choke, then hauled hard on the starter; with a puff of blue smoke, the Johnson chuffed to life on the first crank. I waved goodbye to Loris, who would take my four-wheel drive Suzuki and the boat trailer to meet me on the other side of Bayfield at beautiful Port Superior.

I'd be there in four or five hours, I told her confidently.

Slowly I motored out through the breakwaters and into Siskiwit Bay. Once I was past the pier end, there was little question of what I was in for: A big wave came along, the boat's bow went up, then down, and the outboard's prop spun helplessly in the air, lifted out of the water. A second later, it dug back in, and we were off for the beginning of our rough ride.

Water splashed back along the deck, some spray reaching my face and fogging my glasses. Away from land, and exposed to the wind, I was beginning to feel chilled.

My plan would keep me in the open waters of the lake only while I headed north. When I rounded Point Detour and headed in an easterly direction down the West Channel, I'd be in the Apostle Islands and thus gain some shelter from the northeast winds. I'd follow the channel past Raspberry Island, Oak Island and Basswood Island, and I'd meet Loris to the south of Bayfield at Port Superior.

We seemed to be using a lot of gas punching our way into the wind and waves. After an hour or so, I glanced down at the fuel gauge: it was half empty. This was alarming, though I carried another full tank of gas on board.

Ahead was the passage between Sand Island and the mainland, which shallowed in places down to only about four feet. A cruising guide warned that passages in this channel should be attempted in calm conditions. I was not overly concerned, for *Persistence* had plenty of clearance, since all I had to do was haul up the centerboard. But I knew the effect of water over shallow bars: it made the waves grow large.

The boat was thrashing its way through the oncoming whitecaps, bow slamming into the wave front, splashing water back at me. My glasses were constantly misted over and my face wet.

I put my tiller into an elastic line that would hold course for a few minutes, and I went below to put on even heavier clothing, including wool socks.

Off to my left lay Eagle Island, the westernmost of the Apostle Islands. Today it looked mostly like a wind-whipped, wave-thrashed bleak cluster of rocks. As I finally entered the desolate Sand Island passage, I saw in the distance the first vessel I'd seen out all day, a small powerboat. I waved.

As it went past, my outboard died. I tried restarting it without luck.

I checked the gas tank — I had run out of gas!

There was nothing to do, in the midst of the waves, but to try to pour gas from one engine gas tank into another. The boat bucked, and I had only a small funnel I had cut out of the top of a plastic milk bottle. It helped — but the boat's motion made a mess of the job. Soon, I had poured all the extra gas I had into the Johnson's tank. I had not even counted on using it, but just holding it as spare.

What was going on, anyway? Was the ten horsepower engine, with its twin cylinders, that much more of a gas guzzler than my broken one-cylinder five-horsepower? Whatever the case, I'd have to conserve fuel. I throttled back.

I glanced at my watch. I was now behind schedule, still facing high seas and high winds. But once I rounded Point Detour, passing Sand Island, and got opposite York Island, I'd have some protection. Moreover, I'd be able to hoist sails and turn off the outboard, saving the gas for my final entry to the marina later in the day.

I was wet and chilled, my glasses constantly fogging up. Passing by Sand Island, and then York Island, I turned into the West Channel. The wind was now on our port beam; I raised sails. What a relief to turn off the noisy engine and have the wind propel us along, letting *Persistence* become the wind machine it was.

We sailed gloriously for about a half hour, and then the wind switched to a southeasterly direction — the very direction I wanted to head. I tried tacking the boat — sailing at an angle to the wind — but I just couldn't make much headway.

I checked my watch again, shaking my head. By this time, I should have been in Port Superior to meet Loris. What was she thinking about? I had told her not to worry, that I couldn't predict the weather, and she was a veteran sailor. Still, it would be impossible for her not to be somewhat concerned and probably pacing along the pier, looking for us.

I turned on the engine and tried motor sailing. This helped a bit, but soon the sails were just slowing us down; the wind seemed bent on coming out of the direction I wanted to go, making even motorsailing impossible.

I checked my fuel gauge again. A cold feeling crawled over

my stomach as I realized that in the process we had used up most of our fuel. I did not have enough to make it into the harbor tonight.

I was now in Red Cliff Bay. Basswood Island lay off my port bow. I scanned the waters; I had seen few boats out on this windy day. Off in the distance, I saw one heading in the direction of Schooner Bay.

I turned on my VHF radio. "This is the sailboat *Persistence*,"I announced over the airwaves to anyone listening, "and I am trying to reach the sailboat now about to enter Schooner Bay. I need some assistance." I repeated the message once again, this time adding I was low on gasoline. I hoped the other skipper was listening.

Suddenly, the radio crackled. It was Lew Wolfe in his motor sailor; soon, he, his wife, and their two cocker spaniels were looking down at me. He jumped to his dinghy, being towed behind his boat, and we transferred gas to my outboard tank.

I thanked him profusely and, at the same time, thanked my lucky stars. I was about to resume my voyage when I saw a large white boat with a red stripe down its side motor toward me at speed.

"Do you require assistance?" a polite uniformed Coast Guardsman asked, coming alongside. "We heard your call for gasoline and we were in the area."

"I'm OK now, thanks," I answered. "I have some gas from this boat," I added, feeling embarrassed at all fuss I had caused. "But thanks again," I said. I felt slightly stupid, too, at being caught without enough gas to make it back to port. It was little comfort to know that if I had had my own engine I would have had fuel enough to spare and cruise for several weeks in the Apostles. How was I to know that the ancient Johnson would burn so much precious gas?

With a friendly wave from its crew, the Coast Guard cutter moved smartly off, leaving me alone again.

The long shadows of late afternoon were crawling over Bayfield as I motored past. The sun was setting; I worried about Loris. That would be the hard part: the waiting.

At about 7 p.m., I rounded a wooded point and headed into

Pike's Bay when I saw a light on the end of a pier. It was beautiful Port Superior, and, there waving her arms and with a huge grin on her face, was Loris.

I waved back, happy to be heading for dry land — and to see her again.

She motioned toward the marina, and minutes later, we had *Persistence* tied up along the main bulkhead, just outside the Port Superior Charter Office.

The long day was over.

I had made it, but just barely — with the help of an elderly outboard, some extra gas, and several helping hands.

PART TWO

INTERLUDE
IN THE
ISLANDS

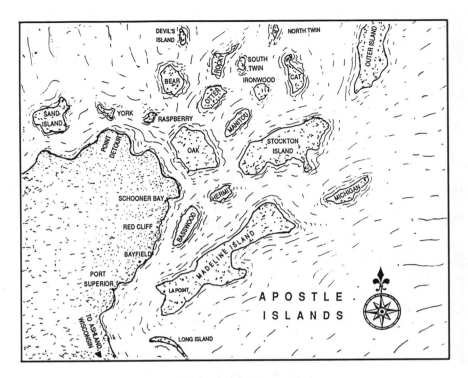

The map shows the Apostle Islands including:
DEVIL'S ISLAND, NORTH TWIN, OUTER ISLAND, ROCKY, SOUTH TWIN, BEAR, IRONWOOD, CAT, OTTER, SAND ISLAND, YORK, RASPBERRY, MANITOU, POINT DETOUR, OAK, STOCKTON ISLAND, MICHIGAN, SCHOONER BAY, HERMIT, RED CLIFF, BASSWOOD, BAYFIELD, MADELINE ISLAND, PORT SUPERIOR, LA POINT, TO ASHLAND WISCONSIN, LONG ISLAND

APOSTLE ISLANDS

CHAPTER THREE

SOJOURN IN THE BEAUTIFUL ISLANDS

THE WIND WAS OUT OF THE SOUTH, southeast, the way I liked it, and the day was another one of Lake Superior's golden kind, with high sunshine glinting on blue water. Superior lapped beyond the harbor's breakwaters, and off in the distance, I could see Madeline Island.

Leisurely, I worked atop the cabin of my wooden boat, tied securely alongside the bulkhead at Port Superior. Eventually I realized I was doing more puttering than actually accomplishing anything and so I put my screwdriver down and just sat atop my little boat, rocking with her in the harbor swells, thinking, reminiscing and anticipating.

After all our adventures so far, just sitting was fine with me. We had arrived. This would be "home" for my boat this summer. In the days ahead, I would be sailing throughout the

Apostle Islands, getting to know this area better. Later on, I would board a cruising catamaran and sail nearly the length of the lake, from Port Superior to Sault Ste Marie, better known as the Soo, on the Canadian side. But for now, I could sit contentedly in the harbor and just rock.

I looked about and I saw that I surrounded by sailboats, all of them bigger than mine: Sloops, cutters, and even a few big catamarans. Some had just come back into harbor after spending time cruising among the islands. Others were waiting patiently at their berths to go out. I studied their details and their lines, for I love sailboats — they fascinate me always.

You meet interesting people by being around sailboats. I sometimes think of a boat's cockpit as being like an old-fashioned front porch, the kind that small towns used to have, where neighbors could get together and talk a spell. In the harbor, being on board a boat gives you a time and a place for small conversational innocence and boaty curiosities. Maybe the fact that the boat rocks slowly in the water provides it with a special relaxing effect, with a sense of leisure and, perhaps, a sort of grace.

I seldom meet a sailboater I do not like. Sometimes I talk to them on their boats, or, at other times, they stop by and chat with me. "What a beautiful little boat," someone will say, and then we'll start talking about sailing, boats, and Lake Superior. It is almost a habit to ask about the weather, whether you are going out, or just coming in, and from there you are into your conversation. It is for me the best part of being around other boaters, and it often brightens my day, for in the cockpit, we are all of the community of boat.

Often the tidbits you learn are not big, but they have a fascination all their own. They put an odd grace in your day. Somehow, because people here are concerned with boats, they are different from what you would find in your normal suburbia. I have met many with affection and respect, including those who are the wise counselors of the Big Lake.

Dave Nixon is one of these. He is chartermaster of Superior Charters at Port Superior, which is one of the largest sailing organizations in the United States berthed in a single harbor.

Since I was tied up beside the bulkhead just outside the chartering office, I constantly saw Dave moving energetically around the docks, helping charterers get into and out of their slips and dispensing useful information. Dave is also a rescuer of boats.

It seems incongruous that on a lake as vast and powerful as Superior that so few chartering fatalities occur, but perhaps that has to do with the chartermasters and the chartering organizations and the quality of the boats they put into service. Still, the lake is unpredictable and occasionally boaters do get caught, in which case, Dave is one of the people who is qualified to provide towing or rescue service.

"We just towed that boat off the northeast side of Rocky Island," Dave told me one day, nodding his head toward the travelift. I turned my head: there, secure in a steel cradle, rested a 29-foot C&C, but even at a glance, I could see all was not well with the big sailboat.

"He was anchored out with two anchors," Dave explained, "when during the night a vicious northeaster blew up, dislodging the anchors and causing the boat to go aground. The skipper immediately started the engine in an attempt to stay off the lee shore. One of the anchor rodes wrapped around the shaft, disabling the engine. Luckily, the other anchor reset. Had that not occurred, the boat most certainly would have been blown up on the rocky shore."

I walked over to the boat, and I could see that the rudder had been torn off and was lying on the ground. That could be replaced with a new one. I checked the lead keel: its damage could be fixed, too, probably by grinding it smooth and filling in the dents. It is sometimes amazing what one can get by with in boats. It also occurred to me that these boaters had been both unlucky — and lucky.

I shook my head, wonderingly. Lake Superior really is a special world, I reminded myself, and I reflected on why I kept returning to Superior.

The attraction has always been there. I am fascinated with a huge body of water so large it seems to possess its own climate; it is the shining inland ocean upon whose huge waters one can actually see the curve of the earth. It has a mystical quality that I have found nowhere else.

Here is not only the scent of fresh water in my nostrils but a presence in my senses and in my mind. It is one of the powerful places on this earth. To walk upon its pine-laden, rocky shores is to sense the footsteps of Hiawatha and the legends of yore. Clambering among its rocks, I am in one of the most ancient places in the world — still as primitive as it was eons ago. Its 2,900-mile shoreline is still relatively wild and untamed — an estimated 92 percent undeveloped. It is as pristine, in many places, as it was when the first European explorers saw it nearly 300 years ago.

Superior is a huge lake, actually, the world's largest freshwater lake by surface volume, with 31,700 square miles of water. It is also the deepest, highest and coldest of the Great Lakes. It alone contains 10 percent of all the surface freshwater in the world. Someone once figured out that if Superior were ever to empty out completely that its water would cover all of the United States, all of Canada and all of Central and South America to a depth of one to two feet.

There is one more distinction: Superior is, to me, the last great lake. It remains the largest body of freshwater in the U.S. that is as yet still relatively unpolluted and still wild and free.

I shook my head: though I was enjoying the lake, I still had things to accomplish. My first order of business was getting a motor. One does not go anywhere on Superior without an engine, and a mighty reliable one.

I checked around; no, the outboard that I had wrecked several days ago could not be fixed locally. I returned the old Johnson outboard to the kind soul who lent it to me in the first place — he'd need his kicker back as spare engine and backup when he went out on Superior. What to do?

I was at wit's end until I heard...

"I've got one!" Joe Boland stepped forward. Joe was the master of the cruising catamaran, *Tullamore Dew*, that we'd sail across Superior. He and his son, Dave, were walking past my boat when they heard of my problems.

"It just came in, never been used before," Joe explained. It was to be the motor for the inflatable boat he carried on the cruising cat. We walked with Dave Nixon to Dave's storage shed, where we took it out of its shipping case. It was a five horsepower — exactly what I liked to have on *Persistence*.

"Let's try it out," I said to Loris, and soon we were underway. The small Mercury had nearly the same kick, or so it seemed to me, as the old 10-horsepower Johnson. We motored out of the harbor, and into the lake. There we were able to set sail and begin enjoying our stay in the Apostle Islands.

We sailed to Madeline Island for lunch and to stretch our legs, and then sailed on to several of the other islands. As we cruised along, enjoying the water and the islands, I was reminded of how interesting this area of Superior is. Historically, it is one of the first settled by the earliest explorers, and was once the home of the early voyageurs. Madeline is the only island that is inhabited year round on the lake; Bayfield is like a beautiful New England town, situated on a hill leading down to the water's edge, ending in row upon row of boats. And I began to think of all the stories I had heard and had come to know about. Some had become intertwined with my own life.

I looked out over the side of the cockpit to the north, where a fog had settled in patches in the islands. There was a magical quality about this area now, a romantic feeling emanating from the grays of sky and water, that brought a sense of nostalgia.

I was reminded of another voyage on Superior, a special vessel, a dream — and a ghost.

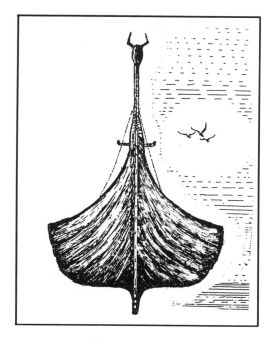

CHAPTER FOUR

THE LONG VOYAGE
OF THE
HOMECOMING SHIP

IN THE MISTS FAR OUT ON THE LAKE, beyond the low-lying clouds, a golden ship ghosted along. From her wooden deck arose a single, towering mast, with square-cut sails filling in the wind. War shields were lashed along her rails, and near the water's edge were oar holes for rowers. Rearing high above the long ship's bow was a carved dragon, surveying the dark seas ahead

She was called the *Hjemkomst* — and from her beginning she was fated for an unusual adventure. The dreams of millions went with her — and some say a ghost rode along, too.

I first heard about the Viking ship and her builder by accident. I was with sailor Gerry Spiess, who had just finished sailing the North Atlantic in his 10-foot boat, *Yankee Girl*. We were working on what was to become a national best-selling book, *Alone Against the Atlantic*, when we were interrupted by a long-distance telephone call from Robert Asp.

"He's a teacher," Gerry explained. "And he has been in the north woods cutting down a hundred white oak trees to build a ship."

The name he gave his boat was the *Hjemkomst*. It meant, "the homecoming."

What the teacher wanted to do was to build a ship patterned after a 1,000-year-old Viking vessel and sail it out of Lake Superior and across the North Atlantic — all the way to his ancestors' home in Norway.

Asp, a junior high school counselor from Moorhead, Minnesota, began building his boat in 1971. With his family and some close friends, he went into Minnesota's north woods to pick out one by one the trees that would furnish the timber for the strange vessel. He cut down the trees, trimmed them, and dragged the logs to a local sawmill, where he had the white oak ripped into planks. He rented a former potato warehouse to begin building his ship.

A perfectionist, Asp wanted his "homecoming ship" to be as close as he could make it to the specifications of the 1,000-year-old Viking ships. He followed the ancient shipbuilder's techniques; except for the use of some power tools, the ship's general details matched those of the original Vikings' ships.

The vessel became a testament to the tenacity and the dream of the teacher working largely alone in the dark, cold warehouse. It was long and tedious work, but slowly, from his hands, the ship grew. The keel he laid was massive — 15 inches thick. The long oak planks were fashioned of one-inch thick oak, then lapped on top of one another. He drove in nearly 7,000 rivets by hand, one at a time.

At times, his children, friends, students and faculty members from the junior high school in Moorhead came to the potato warehouse to help him. Eventually, the *Hjemkomst* reached its full proportions of 76 1/2 feet in length overall and 17 feet in width. Its strong mast rose 60 feet above the deck to carry a square-rigged sail. It would be powered only by the sail and long oars. Fully equipped, it would weigh nearly 20 tons — a massive, magnificent vessel.

In 1980, the old boatbuilder launched his vessel on Lake Superior to begin testing her for seaworthiness and the long voyage ahead. But he was weakening as his boat grew stronger. A few months after his vessel's keel touched the cold waters of Superior, he died of leukemia.

The *Hjemkomst* faced a crisis: would the homecoming ship ever sail again — let alone fulfill her creator's dream?

For a while, the ship stayed in storage. But the teacher had built a legacy of more than a ship: his wife, Rose, and their sons and daughter had been caught up in his homecoming dream. They knew little or nothing about sailing, the North Atlantic, or handling the ancient Viking ship their father had created, but the family's faith and trust in him and his creation was complete.

They vowed to sail the *Hjemkomst* in his stead to Norway.

When the *Hjemkomst* was trucked to Minneapolis to be a part of a festival, I was invited to go on board. I was aghast: Down below, cracks had formed in her massive keel; her bilge was open to the rains and had water pooling in it; several laminated pieces had swollen and split where the epoxy glue had not held. There were cracks in the some of the structural laminations that especially worried me.

I looked at the rudder — essentially a long oar held on at the stern of the vessel. How could this hold such a massive vessel on course? I looked at its fastening, a single bolt. Was this strong enough for the North Atlantic? And the single square sail — thousands of years out of date.

I saw holes in the sides of the hull. These, I was told, were oar holes — so that the crew members could row when the wind failed.

I asked, "How high are these above the water line?"

A crew member held up his hand to measure. "About 12 inches."

I felt a sinking feeling; I had crossed the North Atlantic several times. On a voyage to Britain, a fierce storm had sprung up. The large ship I was on had rocked about in the waves and winds. Green water had gushed down the deck — and that deck was at least 50 feet from the water. These oar holes, just inches above the waterline, could sink the *Hjemkomst*.

Frankly, the whole project looked shaky. The boatbuilder was gone, and without his care, the hull was starting to deteriorate. The vessel itself was an untried boat of ancient design that no one really knew how to sail, and what was even worse, it had a wholly amateur crew.

As I walked away, a friend joshed: "This is your big chance for a ride. Want to volunteer?"

I shook my head. Not only did I not want to go, I was very concerned for the crew.

Yet the dream of the old boatbuilder lingered. This was not just any ship — it was a Viking vessel! The Vikings had been among the most able seafarers in the world, boldly voyaging to the very ends of the earth. Had they not crossed and recrossed the North Atlantic, to establish an early colony in the New World 500 years before Columbus officially discovered it?

I tried to imagine what it would have been like voyaging on that type of double-ended vessel. Judging from what I saw on board the *Hjemkomst*, life must have been pretty miserable. She was open to the skies: every bit of rain, every storm, must have tormented the men on her decks. There would have been no escape from the weather since the vessel had no shelter for her crew either in cabins or below-deck quarters.

Still, for their day, the vessels were marvels of design: the long ships sailed far, crossing oceans and continents. Robert Asp must have experienced some of the power of this kind of ship. He must have felt it as his boat grew during the long, cold vigils he kept in the north woods and in his potato warehouse.

It must have seized him early on, never leaving. And drove him.

How had it all begun? As the story went, Robert Asp fell off a roof, injuring himself. But lying in his hospital bed one day, he talked to his brother, Bjarne, about his dream: building a Viking vessel — to sail to the old country. He began reading books about the Viking vessels, collecting designs and gathering ideas. Together they began preliminary work.

When his brother died, Asp carried on alone. He decided that the vessel would be an exact replica, as nearly as he could make it, of the ancient vessels. He would sail his ship back to the Norway of his ancestors — carrying the dream that he, his brother, and so many others had brought with them to the north woods and the shores of Superior.

Surely, the ancient design carried with it some magic. If in the hands of the Vikings of yore, this vessel could cross oceans and reach across the unknown, then surely it would respond to his hands and those of a his crew.

There were some who said that Asp was mad. He had erred, they said, building not just a Viking vessel — but the wrong design.

The graceful lines of the *Hjemkomst*, it was repeatedly pointed out, came not from the hard-voyaging vessels of Viking lore and history, but from the Gokstad funeral boat.

The potato warehouse boatbuilder had picked the sweeping, almost sensuous lines of a thousand-year old vessel, which had been unearthed from a funeral mound and was now preserved in a museum in Norway. That boat's only function was to be a bearer of the body of a Viking chieftain — a grave ship for his Viking burial.

No, the gossips said repeatedly, the homecoming ship was a replica of the *funeral vessel*, at best a shallow-draft coasting ship, and not meant to put to sea at all.

What the boatbuilder should have built was the more bluff-bowed, deeper and wider Viking raider ship, the Drakkar. This was the type of long ship that had carried the Vikings across the North Sea to terrorize the ancient world; it was a proven design.

Most shook their heads. His beautiful boat was doomed.

From across the seas, Norwegian Captain Erik Rudstrom heard the story of the remarkable homecoming boat.

Captain Rudstrom, at age 61, was an experienced sailor, but in particular, he had sailed a somewhat similarly designed ship, a Femboring, from Norway to Iceland. He was familiar with the Femboring's ways, for it was still revered and used in the old country, often for fishing craft. What was significant was that the Femboring is the modern-day equivalent of the ancient Viking design, and, through it, he knew the secrets of the ancient windships.

He would take the helm of the *Hjemkomstt* — and sail her home.

In Superior's cold waters, the *Hjemkomst* began sea trials under Captain Rudstrom's skilled hands, with the Asp family and friends as crew. She could sail, he readily determined, but modifications had to be made to make her seaworthy.

She was hauled ashore into a little marina carved into a rocky promontory on Superior's north shore, and the work began. He and the crew spent part of one summer rebuilding her massive ship-long keel with heavy steel bolts and deepening it by 12 inches for a bigger grip on the water when going to windward.

The oar holes near the waterline were plugged with coverings, which could be unfastened when the need came to row. The tiller and rudder were entirely rebuilt. The mast was lengthened; now *Hjemkomst* could spread more canvas to catch the trade winds of the North Atlantic. Her sail plan was redesigned; there would be a topsail in addition to the lower sail.

Down below, in the shallow bilge, the crew stowed a whopping eight tons of Superior granite — rocks for ballast, to make her stand up in a blow.

The *Hjemkomst* would have to cross half a continent, three Great Lakes and then, finally, sail 3,500 miles across the North Atlantic to Oslo, Norway.

The crew began hardening themselves physically and mentally for the long voyage. In the heavy rains of spring, 1982, the crew worked up to 16 hours a day, readying Bob Asp's dream. A reporter who visited them noticed they had lobster-red hands from the cold, and that their layers of wool military uniforms, purchased because they were inexpensive but warm, smelled like dead fish.

There were 13 in the crew, including three of Bob Asp's sons, Roger, Tom and Doug, and a daughter, Deborah. There was the white-bearded, silver haired Norwegian skipper, Erik Rudstrom, and two other sailors from Norway, Bjorne Holtet and Vegard Heide. There was Mark Hilde, Jeff Solum, Dennis Morken, Lynn Halmrast, Paul Hesse, and Myron Anderson.

Some say there was a fourteenth member: the spirit of the boatbuilder himself, Robert Asp.

If the crew had any doubt about the ship, they kept it to themselves, believing that the hand of the builder had not erred and that his vision would live.

Not everyone shared their belief. The vessel was open to the skies and the seas, the critics pointed out, and a storm would quickly board the long, undecked vessel, sending her to a watery grave. The ship was not self-bailing, as modern designs were; if any water came on board, it went straight into the bilge instead of running off the decks.

How could they even pump the long bilge? What would happen in the wracking of the waves on the shell-like hull, which lacked the encircling strength of an enclosed deck? Would the boat not twist itself to pieces in the North Atlantic's fierce waves?

And what of the dangers of mighty Superior, the dreaded Great Lake whose storms were notorious? Amateur yachtspeople and residents warned them repeatedly not to go out in a northeaster.

They had only tested their vessel in the warmth of deep summer, when the lake had been relatively calm. As boatbuilder Robert Asp had said, "we were all kind of scared of it."

Captain Rudstrom had no illusions about Lake Superior. He called it a "sea," and he knew of its unforgiving ways on an untested ship and untried crew. He also had plenty of dockside advisors' unsolicited advice: to hug the coastline and be ready to duck into port whenever one of Superior's storms threatened on the horizon.

But he was a man with a mission; he had no inclination to pay attention to storm stories. "We will go straight across the middle of the sea," he announced.

The voyage began from Superior's North Shore on May 11, 1982. The departure from Knife River harbor had been delayed because of easterly winds — the square-rigged *Hjemkomst* could not sail into them.

Finally, after the winds shifted to a northwesterly direction, the vessel began moving at about four or five knots. The second night out, the wind switched to the northeast — and the crew was about to find out what that meant on Superior.

Bjorne Holtet had been asleep inside a tent-like structure behind the mast when he suddenly found himself "swimming
around" in his sleeping bag. A wave had come on board,
sweeping across the deck and inside the tent where Bjorne lay
sleeping.

Floundering about, he jumped up with a cry — to find that
the boat was overcanvassed — pushing the big ship too hard in
a wind of between 20 to 30 knots.

The boat's lee rail dipped below the waves, scooping up solid green water. Each time that happened, a few hundred gallons of icy water sluiced across the deck and ran down into the bilges.

The ship was in danger. Quickly, he and the crew reefed the sail, slowing the ship down and straightening her up a precious few degrees, letting the weather rail come up out of the water. They pumped the bilge to get out the water, and replugged the oar holes.

Exhausted and wet, the off-duty shift then crawled back into their cold, damp sleeping bags to get what comfort they could. They had passed their second night on Superior.

The ship picked up speed in the strong winds, carrying the *Hjemkomst* eastward at about five knots under steely gray but rainless skies. They relied entirely on their square sail to drive them, using their oars to help turn the ship through the wind. They were cold and wet — Superior was challenging them.

As they passed the Apostle Islands, their course led to the northeast, up and around the Keweenaw Peninsula — into the teeth of the May wind.

They began a series of tacks, back and forth in a zig-zag pattern. Progress was slow; there was dense fog and intermittent rain.

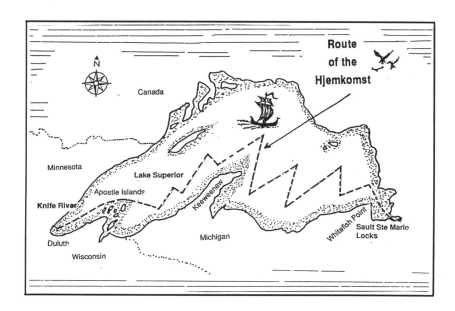

They pumped out the bilge, then lifted by hand the rocks they used as ballast, moving some from the bow to the stern to raise the forward part of the hull so that it would ride higher. In that way, they reasoned, waves and spray wouldn't come into the boat as much.

They also stuffed more material into the oar holes to keep water out. They came close to losing their dragonhead, which they had named Igor, when a wave knocked it down.

The open boat was pure misery. There was no heat on board. A small canvas cabin they erected was to have been warmed by a compact coal-burning stove. But since the stove burned coal, and not the charcoal briquettes they carried, the fire had to be started by kindling. None had been brought aboard. The diesel stove that was to be the cookstove also would not light; the crew finally successfully tried a propane torch.

The boat's long keel made it difficult to maneuver; they had problems tacking high enough to clear Michigan's Keweenaw Peninsula. The square sail was hard to set correctly; it didn't want to tack into the wind.

For days, they zig-zagged against persistent headwinds and rain squalls, ever onward toward the locks at Sault Ste. Marie. Drenching rain and Superior's 38-degree water kept them wet; they began to fantasize about hot meals of steak and eggs.

On the morning of May 18, eight days after leaving the western shores of Superior, they reached the southeastern tip of the lake and entered the Sault Ste. Marie locks.

Because of the stubborn headwinds and the northeaster, one crew member estimated that instead of covering about 400 miles, they had sailed close to 700. Later, some of the crew said that the voyage across Lake Superior was the toughest part of the entire trip.

Crossing Lake Huron was a breeze, by comparison. They whipped their Viking ship down the lake in around 30 hours of sailing.

By now, the cities of the Great Lakes had caught the spirit of the Viking vessel. Bells, whistles and cheering crowds greeted them as they entered ports with pennants flying at the masthead. The craft made good time through Lake Erie to the Erie

Canal. A rowing club showed up, volunteering to row the vessel through. In Albion, New York, school classes were let out to come down to watch the vessel as it glided along the canal.

Hjemkomst crew members blew the Viking horn as the ship neared a bridge; from atop, well-wishers sometimes lowered baskets of fruit, food, or wine. From one bridge came a shower of T-shirts imprinted with the cryptic phrase, "Viking Valhalla Room."

Majestically, pennants flying, the *Hjemkomst* sailed proudly down the Hudson River to New York City. Her berth would be one of honor: New York City's historic South Street Seaport, on the East River.

But as she neared the George Washington bridge, media helicopters repeatedly flew over the windship. The downwash not only splashed the harried crew, but the blasts of air filled the sail from different directions, making keeping a course difficult.

Someone shouted, "Look out!"

With a cracking noise, the ship collided with a steel bridge piling. A heavy oak plank had cracked partly along its length on the port side. This was serious damage to the hull. But it was above the water line.

The ship put in at the South Street Seaport in lower Manhattan, in the shadow of the skyscrapers. The seaport's historic windships' massive hulls and four masts dwarfed the smaller wooden ship. At the dock, visitors peered down at the Viking ship.

They had braved Superior and its storms, crossed the Great Lakes and made it to the Big Apple.

But problems continued. A fire broke out as the crew members prepared lunch: the diesel stove had flared up. Ship's master Roger Asp was burned along his right forearm; as he fell to the deck, another crew member poured a pail of water — which was standing by to have been used for heating hot dogs — over him, dousing the fire. The crew member was also burned on his leg. They had been lucky, though. The fire had been near other flammable materials, which had not ignited.

The crew began making repairs, cleaning up the mess created

by a fire extinguisher, and also the damage caused by the fire to the ship's minimal electrical wiring. They also repaired the damaged planking. Instead of replacing the cracked strake, they decided to "sister" the damaged area by fastening another plank over it, in effect, bracing it from the inside. They hoped the fastening would hold across the Atlantic.

There was one last problem. Crew member Lynn Halmrast was on shore to buy a going-away gift to send to his son. He decided on a miniature ship, but as he held it in his hand, turning it over, fear struck him. He began to worry that this could be the last toy he'd ever buy for his son.

With tears in his eyes, he made a difficult decision: He would leave the voyage. He would not be a hero, but he would be a father to his son.

The thirteenth member was gone; the crew now stood at twelve.

With their Viking figurehead proudly guiding the way, they sailed out of New York harbor on June 14 to enter the Atlantic Ocean. Suddenly, the whole sea was theirs. The problems of civilization lay behind them; their horizons were open. They were sailors on a historic crossing of the North Atlantic.

By the 20th, dark clouds had overtaken them, and the barometer kept dropping. The wind increased to nearly 40 knots, and waves began marching onto the vessel. They were in their first Atlantic storm.

At 1 a.m., the crew was roused to lower the sail — almost too late. Under the pressure of the relentless wind, the Viking vessel heeled so far that the starboard gunnel was shipping water. But the big sail wouldn't slide down — the fierce wind was keeping it up. Finally, they had to wrestle the sail down by hand.

Dawn came with dangerous waves. But the wind had abated somewhat; the crew wanted to get moving again and so they hoisted the reefed sail.

The *Hjemkomst* flew along. Suddenly, she overran one big wave. Her big hull reached over the crest and went airborne in the forward section, slamming down with a shock — and a cracking noise. Water gurgled in the bilge; someone checked below: They had a whopping 14-foot-long crack in one plank.

They bailed, stuffed the crack, and sailed on.

Now the winds were giving them a real ride, and the long, straight hull was showing its seafaring heritage, flying over the waves. The hull flexed and bent, snaking its way through the waves — the way the ancient shipwrights had designed this vessel. At times it went so fast that the hull waves wrapped around the aft section of the vessel, continuously dousing the helmsman.

The sea they had feared was now the vessel's natural element, rather than its enemy; the boat lived up to their father's dream. There was not a place on deck that was dry. Their food began to mold, their drinking water tasted of sea salt. They passed Britain and entered the North Sea, seeming to move faster as their destination neared.

Then, after 34 days at sea, the homecoming ship arrived in Norway.

As the *Hjemkomst* entered Bergen Harbor on the 19th of July, nearly 600 vessels came out to greet her. Drummer boys beat drum rolls as each of the crew disembarked to stand on Norwegian soil. A band played the anthems of the United States and Norway. Flags flying, the people of Norway joyously welcomed the Viking ship as if it were a long lost relative returning to its home shores.

In the midst of the festivities, the boatbuilder was not forgotten. Captain Rudstrom asked for a moment of silence for the man whose ghost seemed to ride on the ship. Heads bowed, the crew and the crowd remembered Robert Asp.

Triumphantly, the *Hjemkomst* began her tour of her beloved land. Cheers and greetings came from shore everywhere she was seen. The ship and the crew were heroes.

King Olaf of Norway came in his own ship to see the Viking vessel and the crew went on board the king's yacht to hear his congratulations. But when they returned to the *Hjemkomst* after about a half hour, they made a startling discovery. The vessel was riding so low in the water that even her floor boards were floating. The crack had begun opening up, and in their celebrating they had not kept pumping the vessel.

As the King watched and waved, the crew began bailing out the water by hand. When his ship sailed away, they started the bilge pumps. Slowly, the water exited and the ship rose.

It had been a close call.

The final part of the homecoming journey took the ship and crew to Oslo. Flags flying, a flotilla of boats and ships came out to greet them. Thousands of well wishers crowded the shore.

The ship that had begun life in a potato warehouse docked at the Pier of Honor, reserved for the ships of the king and other dignitaries. It was a huge welcome for the first Americans to cross the Atlantic in a Viking vessel.

There were tears in the eyes of the crew members as they, and their homecoming ship, reached the end of their destination.

Today, if you travel to western Minnesota, as I did, you will see among the wooded acres a tall structure that looks like two huge white tents pitched end to end. Upon a closer look, they might even seem to resemble sails.

This remote location near the banks of the Red River, so far away from big water, may be an unlikely place for a Viking ship to end its days. The *Hjemkomst* never sailed the North Atlantic again, but came back to the U.S. on the deck of a freighter. As you enter the Heritage-Hjemkomst Interpretive Center, at Moorhead, you'll see her hull's golden wood gleaming, her tall mast rising up nearly to the ceiling of the sail-like roof.

Now thousands of visitors, including many school children, come to see this boat that one man constructed largely by himself in a nearby potato warehouse. Some of them grow misty eyed as they dream of the sea and the watery path to a distant homeland.

They know, too, as they gaze upon the *Hjemkomst*, that one man's dreams did come true.

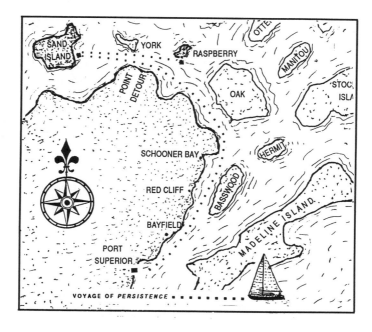

CHAPTER FIVE

VOYAGE TO
TWO ISLANDS

Our DESTINATION TODAY was an island I had wanted to visit
for some time. Sand Island was one of the outermost of the
Apostle Islands to the west and one of the most remote to
sailors. It had always held a special attraction for me.

In 1984, I had first sailed around the island during my solo
voyage on the western shores of the big lake. Coming up the
West Channel, I had headed around Eastern Bay, past the lighthouse which formed the westernmost light of the Apostles,
before setting my course southwestward for Cornucopia. At-
tracted by the island, I had cut in close to scrutinize its rugged
and wild shores. It seemed like an especially interesting island
to visit. Someday.

I had heard stories about Sand Island from a man I met
during my first solo voyage. He told of living on the island as a
boy in the 1930s and how he lost his father when a northeaster
came through. The island had been settled after the Civil War,
when a veteran by the name of Shaw received a land grant on

the island for a veteran's bonus. The village of Shaw developed over the years; settled by many Norwegians, it became a fishing village and sent its fish to nearby Bayfield. In the 1950s, when fishing declined, the village was abandoned.

Today, I was sailing to Sand Island at last. We had a bouncy passage as we rounded Point Detour and passed York Island. But as Loris and I neared Sand, the water turned calmer; with the island to windward, it was shouldering off the breezes. I could smell the pines and the virgin greenery above the freshwater scent of Superior. The voyage over had been chill, with whitecaps, but now it seemed like summer again.

As we came closer, I saw a wonderful golden sand beach, with pines coming nearly down to the water's edge. At the logdock, there was only a single fishing skiff tied up.

I breathed deeply of the island air and was reminded that there is something special about an island. It is hard to define, but an island is unlike any other piece of land, and Sand seemed to be especially welcoming, warm and inviting.

As I tied up, with my bow pointing away from land, I glanced below the hull. We were out of the marine blue of deep water and now in water almost gin-clear down to a golden sand bottom. *Persistence* seemed to be hanging suspended on clear waters, tethered to the dock by a spider-web of lines.

One of my priorities was to visit the lighthouse I had seen on my voyage around the island to the north. It seemed remote, looking out over the miles of water. I knew it was one of six lighthouses in the Apostle Islands, which has a greater concentration of lights than in any other national recreational area. These lights have been guiding ships on their passages throughout the area for a century and a half, and have played a significant role in shipping.

"There's a trail of about two miles through the woods to the lighthouse," one of the park employees told us. He was one of the park people who give time and work in return for the privilege of living on the island during the summer. They had badges proclaiming them to be VIP's, volunteers in the park services.

We began hiking; in a short time, we had gone beyond the beautiful sand beaches into an island wilderness. Here beauti-

ful flowers and wild berries grew in profusion; there was a still-
ness and a fragrance to the air.

"It smells so clean," I remarked to Loris.

Along one section of the path lay rusted remains of several
automobiles — vintage 1920 or so. The park service person had
told us about them: The fishing community, in its heyday, had
several cars on the island but now they were deserted along the
path. At one time there were over 100 persons living here, but
after fishing declined in the 1950s and the last of the stalwart
village moved off Sand Island, the government removed the
old fishing shacks and houses, and let the area return to a
natural state. It is now a part of the Apostles Islands National
Lakeshore.

Part of the path was wooded; where there was marsh or
water, the park service had laid logs. In some areas, the island
was heavy with thickly intertwined trees. On the ground were
lush carpets of flowers and grasses. It was wilderness here —
an untamed frontier. I loved it.

Perspiring but elated, we arrived at the northernmost tip of
the island. Facing the lake was the old lighthouse we had
sought. Sitting near the rocks overlooking the lake was Nancy
Peterson, a volunteer in the park program. She lived here
during the summer. This was her third year on Sand Island and
her second at the lighthouse.

Nancy didn't think it was unusual for a lone woman to be a
lighthouse keeper. "People get lonesome out here," she told
me, but added, "people get lonesome living downtown." She
said that she keeps her mobile radio with her all the time.

I wondered why she settled on the island. "I paddled here
five years ago in a sea kayak," she said. "Sand Island interested
me. I got in touch with the volunteer program, and volunteered."

She had fallen in love with the island and chose to live here
as much as she could, which was summers. She began to show
us her special lighthouse; I could see it was massively built like
a fortress — a castle whose ramparts would keep out the in-
vader, the inland sea, and whose tower would shine a beacon
out to the ships in fog, storms, and night.

I could also see why it was considered the islands' most

scenic lighthouse. It was built of brownstone quarried here in the Apostle Islands, and was constructed in a Norman Gothic style. It had an octagonal light tower, which arose from the northwest corner of the brownstone building.

Inside, the lighthouse was as cool as a bank vault. We ascended the circular steps to the tower, then clambered up a steep iron ladder to the top of the light tower. I tried to imagine what it was like on a stormy night for a lighthouse keeper to ascend these steps to check the all-important light.

From the 56-foot height of the light tower, we took a look around. The big sea sparkled with glittering waves; giant freighters plied the nearby shipping lanes.

It was here that an oil lamp was lighted for the first time in September 1881, and kept its lonely vigil for ships out at sea. But in September, 1905, a tragedy occurred.

"It happened out there," Nancy said, sweeping her arm to indicate the Sand Island shoals about a mile and a half northeast of us. "It must have been from here that the lighthouse keeper saw the wreck of the *Sevona*," she began to explain ominously.

Emanuel Lueck's oil lamp could only emit a weak beam into the wild storm that was raging on Superior. Out there, the Sand Island lighthouse keeper knew, was a ship on the shoals; he could barely see through the spray-drenched glass. Despite its name, Sand Island Shoal was a ridge of solid sandstone.

The ship was the *Sevona*, laden with 6,000 tons of iron ore. The 372-foot steel vessel had steamed out of Superior's harbor on Friday evening, September 1, 1905, on a pleasant night, with no wind but with heavy ground swells, to a weather forecast of good conditions. But the wind began to rise and by midnight it was a full-force Superior gale — a dreaded northeaster. Seas regularly boarded the vessel, running the length of the deck.

Captain Donald Sutherland MacDonald managed to turn the 3,100-ton steamer back to attempt to shelter in the Apostle Islands. As the *Sevona* ran before the gale, Captain MacDonald had two of his passengers, young women, escorted along lifelines through waist-deep waves to the aft of the ship, where the freighter carried her two lifeboats.

In the forward wheelhouse, the captain and the helmsman searched the curtains of rain and the dark for the Sand Island or Raspberry Island lighthouses. But there was no guiding beacon they could make out; they were running blind.

Suddenly, there was a crash, then two more distinct groundings that all could feel. They had struck Sand Island shoal; before their horrified eyes, the *Sevona* broke in two. Pounded on the reef by heavy waves, the ship was helpless.

As light dawned over the raging lake, Captain MacDonald hauled out his megaphone to shout through the wind to direct the men in the aft section. Lower the lifeboats in the protection of the hull, he ordered, but do not let them go in the raging waters. In the bow section, seven men began to make a raft from wooden hatch covers and doors.

The ship fired rocket flares. A mile and a half away, the lighthouse keeper could only watch helplessly as the *Sevona* was pounded and tossed in the 25 to 35-foot high waves.

The northeaster's waves slammed into the lighthouse structure itself, the spray reaching as high as the beacon where the lighthouse keeper kept his vigil. He was unable to help the stricken ship; the *Sevona's* crew had to fend for themselves.

By 11 a.m., the Sand Island lighthouse keeper saw through his binoculars that some of the crew had launched lifeboats from the wrecked hull. They pulled frantically on the oars, but in the roaring waves, it was a desperate fight to keep the small boats afloat. One boat, bailing constantly, swept past the island but eventually came aground on the Wisconsin mainland; the other was blown onto the island.

Lueck's binoculars swung back to the ship. The bow section, which had been holed, now had a list and was battered by waves. He saw Captain MacDonald and his men dash from the wheelhouse to launch their makeshift wooden raft over the side. They clung desperately to the unstable raft as huge breakers roared past, inundating them in the icy storm waters. The men seemed to be hanging on to one another, so that no one would be washed overboard. It appeared they were going to make it.

As the raft neared the island, the breakers grew larger. The raft bucked skyward — then broke up. The men disappeared beneath the waves. Four days later, Captain MacDonald's battered body and those of the other crew members were found along the Sand Island beach.

Some of the remains of the old ship are still out there. I sailed past them years ago; a cruising guide warned to be wary, though the water above the wreck's remains had a minimum depth of 15 feet. The bow section lies in a different area from the stern section, an awesome reminder of Superior's power.

My thoughts were interrupted as our guide continued showing us around the lighthouse tower. As we stood viewing the sun-lit waters over the reef, the scene was all tranquility and beauty. The air was fresh and scented of fresh water.

"It's a wonderful place to live. Such a treat," she added.

Down below, near the water's edge in the rocks, I saw the colored shape of a small boat. "My sea kayak," she said. "I'll use it to run over to the other side of the island this evening," she explained. "It beats walking."

Later that evening, as the sun set, we settled down in *Persistence*, rocking gently on the clear waters. It was a time for adjustment.

There is always a sense of awe which comes over me my first night on a voyage. We were in the shelter of a round, pine-filled island, floating on the tranquil waters of the world's largest freshwater sea. It was beautiful this evening.

There was a huge moon, and I decided to sit with crossed legs on the forward teak deck. I lifted my face to the sky and remained motionless. I could feel the mild breeze out of the southwest. I felt the bob of my boat. Slowly, I was getting in touch and acquiring a sense of place.

Fatigue began overtaking me. I took one more look around, then I walked a few steps aft, my little boat bobbing lightly beneath me. As I closed the cabin hatch I saw Loris was in the bow berth, reading a book. I crawled forward a few feet to be beside her. For two people, and their gear, *Persistence* is small, but supremely comfortable for its size. As I lay down on the soft bunk, I felt wonderfully secure. I reached up to open the wooden hatch just above me. The smell of the water and the island gently wafted in.

I pulled up the sleeping bag. The gentle motion of the boat, tugging on her lines, took over my senses. The water was just inches away from where my head lay; I could hear it gurgling past and could almost feel it. I became a part of my boat, lightly resting on the waters, tugging gently on the lines, then drifting outward a few inches. And then back in a never-ending gentle cycle. Just a boat and crew in rhythm with nature.

Civilization and its burdens seemed ages away. There was a full moon over Superior tonight, rising yellow and turning brilliant white to shine over the dark pines of the islands. It bathed my little boat, floating like a leaf on the water, in its glow.

The next morning, the sun rose high and clear. The sky was pink and blue; there was no wind on our side of the island. A beautiful day beginning. We started with a hearty breakfast.

Today, I began to make a cafe latte, thanks to my newly installed espresso maker. This was one of the marvels of my little boat, and its even tinier galley, and was in part my own creation.

It consisted of a camper's espresso maker, which would make one cup of the thick coffee, when heated over my butane stove. I had solved the problem of how to suspend the fist-sized espresso maker over the stove by using a camp toaster, which was a perforated sheet of metal designed to hold bread over open flames of a camp fire. I had some old-fashioned metal cups, which I partially filled with spoonfuls of powdered milk, to which I added water. I set one of them atop the hot espresso maker.

Even with the torch-like flame from the stove, it took minutes for the espresso to bubble out the tube at the top and into the cup, warming up the milk and also the cup. Once I partially filled one metal mug, I carefully took that off, adding the second metal mug. This way, both Loris and I could enjoy our morning latte.

For our breakfast, I cooked bannock bread, which we ate with strawberry jam.

We shoved off to explore another island — and another lighthouse. Our boating guide warned of rocks off Raspberry Island. Loris went forward to the bow to watch for them as we closed in on the base of the old lighthouse and the pier. From our westerly approach, I could see that the shoreline was steep and heavily forested.

As we neared land, the water cleared and we could see a rocky bottom. Our charts showed that in approaching the dock we needed to be especially aware of the western end of Marina Shoal, which reached out from the island. With *Persistence's* shallow draft, we had no problem coming close.

I was anxious to get on Raspberry Island, for its specially restored light station with its beautiful location, grounds and gardens was once the showcase of the islands. I had admired the lighthouse many times in my cruises through the Apostles. But until now, I had not actually set foot on the island.

The lighthouse, established in 1862, was a guiding light to shipping in the West Channel through the Apostle Islands to Bayfield. The City of Bayfield had been founded only about six years before the lighthouse was built; its deep-water harbor had made Bayfield an important port when the Sault Ste. Marie canal opened Lake Superior to eastern shipping. The lighthouse also helped guide ships in the channel to the Twin Ports of Duluth and Superior, at the head of the lake, then just being developed.

Like the old lighthouse at Sand Island, the Raspberry Island lighthouse is on the National Register of Historic Places. The lighthouse is situated on a hill about 40 feet above the water's edge, and the tower soars above a rectangular frame lighthouse keeper's house. There is an iron walkway surrounding the light station. Inside, the tower light is equipped with a Fresnel lens.

We tied up on a long, wooden dock, then clambered up the steps to the lighthouse. At the top, we met several other boaters who had anchored off the island for the night.

A man in full, but ancient, uniform and who introduced himself as "Toots" came forward to meet us. "You're in luck," he said, pleased with himself. "I just took my Saturday night bath."

"You're not," the boaters responded. "We didn't."

Toots smiled. He was, of course, a seasonal park interpreter, in the role of a 1920's lighthouse keeper. He was re-creating history, and the effect was as if we were in a time warp and somehow had stepped off our boats and had been transported back three-quarters of a century.

"Back in Bayfield, it may be the year 1923," he explained, "but here it could be anytime."

"Did you know," Toots asked with a touch of whimsical admiration, "that they have flush toilets in Bayfield?"

Bayfield was the epitome of civilization to Toot's way of life as a remote 1920's lighthouse keeper. "You pay $1 a night for a room in Bayfield," he pointed out, "and you get three meals for a dollar there, too."

Despite these wonders, there was trouble in the big city. "You look around on Saturday night," he said, "and you see some young guys wearing mascara on their eyes." He shook his head sadly at misguided youth. "They've just seen a Rudolph Valentino movie and are trying to be like that movie star."

We began our tour in the lighthouse, a massively built 20th-century fortress on the outside, spartanly furnished inside. "In Bayfield, they have indoor plumbing," he said, bringing out a galvanized tub. "But I've got this."

"Do you want to try it out?" he asked. We shook our heads.

"Well, it just fits me," Toots said, settling his lanky frame into the small tub. His legs and upper body stuck out, like a stork trying to settle itself in a kettle. He was an awkward picture, yet pleased with himself as he recounted the lighthouses's advanced bathing features: "We collect rain water off the roofs. There are gutters up there and they lead through pipes to the basement. We get our soft water that way."

On a table in the living room, I looked at a book. It was a *World Almanac* dated 1923. At night, Toots read by an oil lamp. A booklet on the table was open to an article headed "President Harding's last public utterances regarding the flag and the *Star Spangled Banner*."

We walked upstairs into a small room that was the emergency bedroom. He bent under the bed to pull out a little pot with a lid on it.

"What is it for?" he asked us, and, not getting an answer, continued: "Just imagine that some night you have to go to the outhouse, and there's a bear between you and it. Well, just forget it."

He held up the little pot again. Now it was obvious what it was for.

Toots carefully put a white glove on his hand. "Did you know that dust is illegal in lighthouses?" he asked, wiping his hand along the top sill of a door. "An inspector comes around with his white gloves; you can get fired if there is dust on his finger."

Despite the strictness of lighthouse regulations, Toots clearly loved his island life.

"It used to be, after I got back from the Great War (World War I) that whenever I heard a car backfire I would nearly jump out of my skin. But out here, it's so peaceful that I've forgotten all about that."

"So you see, I don't mind being behind the times," he added peacefully.

It was with regret that we walked down the long flight of steps to our boat and shoved off for other adventures.

CHAPTER SIX

THE BOAT
THAT WOULD
NOT DIE

SHE LAY BOBBING GRACEFULLY in the slip beside the wooden building that served as a shipyard. As I sailed by, I could see that she was a wooden ship of an older sea-kindly design. Her wooden masts gave a clue to her history: they were dark with age and varnish, weathered by years of salt water. Her bronze fittings were massive and old fashioned; an old wooden steering wheel and entry hatch showed years at sea.

Originally, she was *Shadowfax*, lovingly built in 1928 to a John Alden design, but by the time Mike Caswell and Barb Tellier found her near Annapolis, Maryland, she was down on her luck. Her backbone was badly rotted and she was "hogged" —

she sagged because her keel and stringers no longer had the strength to keep her in shape. After a half century at sea on the Atlantic coast, she was a doomed vessel — that is, until she caught the Bayfield couple's eyes.

I stepped on board and knocked lightly on the hatch, which was open. I had been following the vessel's progress from when it was upside down and its hull being laid up in a large building just off main street in downtown Bayfield. I remembered the occasion well, several years ago, when I had been walking the streets of Bayfield and a building's large sliding door had been open. I had glanced in, and there it was, in all its golden glory: A big wooden boat, of an old-fashioned schooner design. I had walked around it lovingly.

In the spring of 1994, the hull had been moved to the waterfront slip. Today, I was cautious: I had not been invited and boatbuilders were busy people. They answered my knock on the hatch and invited me in. "You don't mind if I talk while I continue working, do you?" Mike asked.

"Not at all," I said. I had, after all, built my own wooden boat from scratch, and I knew how hard Mike would have to keep working, despite interruptions from visitors. I looked around below: the wooden interior shone brightly with varnish and paint.

"I was in love with Alden designs," Mike explained, "and then I saw her."

"And he fell in love with this boat," Barb added.

He continued: "As a boat builder and repairer, I am familiar with what is known as the boat lover's 'conspiracy of optimism.'" He added, "I still fell for her."

Their original plan was to travel to the East Coast, purchase a boat and bring it back to Superior, maybe to put it into the charter trade. In 1991, they found *Shadowfax* to their liking — then made a tough decision.

"It was hard," Mike said. "Making the first cut."

But he fired up his chain saw and cut off 10 feet of her bow.

"*Kerplunk*," he said, reliving the moment, "and it fell off."

Difficult though it was for them to cut up the old boat, Mike and Barb had their plans: they would take everything from the old boat that could be reused — masts, shrouds, yards, wheel, vents, cabinets — and build a new boat around them.

Shadowfax would live again — but this time in the clear, cold waters of Superior. It helped that they found the original 65-year-old plans on the boat.

For three weeks, working day and night, the couple dismantled the boat, saving everything that could rebuild *Shadowfax*, including a 22-foot long, 8,500-pound keel casting. They loaded everything that remained of *Shadowfax* onto a flat-bed trailer and trucked it back to Bayfield.

The first step was to build a new "backbone," the stem and the keel. Unlike the old *Shadowfax*, the schooner that would emerge would be wood glued and sealed with modern-day epoxy.

They called her *Ananda*. To create the hull, the boatbuilders glued long strips of Douglas Fir, 1 1/8 inches by 1 3/4 inches in section, in the strip-plank technique. These strips ran lengthwise along the hull, epoxy glued to each other and to the ribs. The hull was encapsulated in epoxy and covered with a layer of fiberglass, inside and out.

Mike knocked his knuckle against the hull. "When you tap the hull, the whole hull rings — it's one piece," Mike said proudly.

Inside the high-tech monocoque wooden hull the boat-builders carefully added the pieces they rescued from *Shadowfax*. Mike and Barb pointed them out to me: the wooden salon table, a beautiful brass lamp, cabinets, the galley sink. Large panels of wood from the old schooner's cabin were fitted into the beautiful new epoxy-wood hull. They stepped *Shadowfax's* wooden masts and added her hatch covers, vents, steering wheel and fittings.

In about two years, the old schooner had come alive again from bits and pieces into a new boat. And a much stronger one.

Work continued on her even as I strode her belowdecks' area and clambered over her cockpit. Even as they finished her off, she was being taken out for charters and put into service, little bit by little bit.

I moved to the cockpit, then lightly touched the varnished wheel. I looked her over, from her cockpit to the jaunty bow, as her masters had done so many years ago. Her tall wooden masts seemed to reach up to the heavens; her bowsprit jutted jauntily ahead. With her long overhangs and sweeping sheer, she was as graceful as a swan upon the water.

Mike had a far-away look in his eyes, which Barb shared.

"You know, the original boat went around the world," Mike said. "So there is historical precedent. Somebody may charter us to go to Tahiti."

"Or," Barb added, "we may have to reconstruct the original voyage someday."

To my way of thinking, *Ananda* certainly looked strong and capable enough for an around-the-world trip.

After all, she was the boat that would not die.

CHAPTER SEVEN

HUNTERS
OF
LOST SHIPS

THE DAY WAS BRILLIANT SUNSHINE as we sped through the Cornucopia breakwaters and out toward the open waters of Lake Superior. I was in a Zodiac inflatable, powered by a 35-horsepower outboard, and it was my first ride in this remarkable sea sled so favored by SCUBA divers. I was with two divers — and we were on the track of a sunken ship, the *Benjamin Noble*. The swells were out of the north, and we were slamming into them, spray flying everywhere.

"Your first inflatable ride?" diver Kraig Smith, of Rice Lake, Wisconsin, inquired. I nodded uncomfortably. The Zodiac did not immediately inspire my confidence. It is the boat seen on television on the Cousteau odysseys, skidding at high speed over the waves. The Zodiac resembles nothing so much as an oversized black rubber truck inner tube shaped somewhat angularly in the form of a boat. Now I was on board one, heading out to sea.

Suddenly, we were partially airborne.

The feeling of being launched and weightless lasted only seconds; with a jolt, the bow plunged down into the next onrushing wave train. The boat shuddered; spray flew everywhere.

I wiped the water off my glasses with my finger, but I needn't have bothered, for now the boat began a spiral of slams into the incoming waves. I bounced with it, perched on the port "tube" with my left hand wrapped around a rope, balancing on one haunch.

I began looking for a place to get more secure, if not more comfortable. There wasn't any.

"Everybody just sits on the tube," diver Jerry Eliason, of Cloquet, Minnesota, yelled. "You get used to it."

I hunched lower, my body jerking back and forth as the Zodiac punched over the waves. We were just beginning our search, slamming out to sea — and we had a long day ahead of us on Superior.

The clues we were investigating had come to me weeks earlier when I was in an old fishing village. "I don't know what you want to do with this," a retired fisherman had told me, "but we saw something out there."

He and his wife had been in their boat on the way back to the harbor when they noticed something odd on their LCR — the electronic "fishfinder" that most serious sportsfishermen use these days. These remarkable liquid crystal displays, a lot like a television set, showed what was below the boat, such as fish, and what was on the bottom.

That was what fascinated the fisherman and his wife. On their LCR, they saw what appeared to be an old ship below their keel.

"We were on a line with it," he explained. "First we saw the stern section and cabin come into view. Then we were over the long spar deck. And then we clearly saw what looked like the pilot house, with its mast sticking up in the water."

"Did you get a bearing on shore?" I asked.

"No, we were too busy looking at the wreck. But she lies on a line between Bark Point and Squaw Point in 100 feet of water. If you go straight out from the Cornucopia entryway until you hit that depth, then you should be about in a line between the two points. And that's where you'll find her."

It was electrifying news — and it sounded all too good to be true.

No, the experts at the Canal Park Marine Museum told me, there were no known shipwrecks in that harbor — too far off the normal shipping lanes.

Thom Holden, Assistant Curator, said he knew of an old tug that had sunk years ago lying in the depths near the entryway, but other than that, there wasn't anything that they knew about — much less a vessel that had been estimated by the fisherman to be between 300 and 350 feet long.

"That rules out the *Benjamin Noble*," I said. The so-called ghost ship of Superior, I knew, was 239 feet long and was one of western Lake Superior's most fascinating wrecks. She had last been seen somewhere off the Duluth Canal, heading for harbor, but then she disappeared with all hands in a wild spring gale April 28, 1914. The wreck was never found.

"Not necessarily," came the reply. "She could have broken going down, and part of her wreckage could extend out. It has happened before."

"But the *Noble* is thought to lie somewhere within 20 miles of Duluth."

"No one knows. Hatch covers and some of her superstructure washed up on Minnesota Point, but they could have washed down from anywhere."

The facts were elusive: the currents of Superior during a storm were not known to the people I talked to, so that there was no way to pinpoint the sinking. Certain items of wreckage were well scattered. The *Noble's* hatch covers were discovered the day after her sinking, April 28, on the sandy beach of Minnesota Point, at about 30th Street South. Her pilothouse was found further south on the point. Life belts, a life raft, spars, oars and clothing were scattered over a wider area, from not only the Minnesota Point beaches but also along Duluth's north shore, some as far as five miles from the harbor. A fisherman at French River, about 10 miles northeast of Duluth, found a body in his nets a few days later.

All this seemed to indicate to me that the *Noble* had not sunk directly off the canal, as some surmised, but had turned to head back into the teeth of the northeaster. Perhaps she had struggled northward, hoping to find shelter somewhere in the Apostle Islands; maybe she had made it here as far as Siskiwit Bay before her luck ran out. It was just possible. No one knew for certain.

Today, as I hunted for one of western Superior's most famous vanished ships, I tried to imagine what it was like that terrible night on Superior. What must the *Noble's* young captain have felt as he made his fatal command decisions? What must he and the ship have been going through? A scenario came into my mind as I began to recreate the final hours of the *Benjamin Noble*.

The waves were ominous. The surge of the seas lifted the deeply laden ore boat's stern so far out of the water that her huge bronze wheel thrashed in the air, vibrating and shaking the steel ship. Spray blurred the young captain's vision; he could see the *Benjamin Noble's* bow rise, then plunge downward, burying itself in the black waves. Tons of water surged over the bow, rushing back to batter the pilot house. The ship shuddered with each blow.

From behind, fast-moving breakers overtook the laboring vessel and slid over the lifelines along the deck's length, building up like miniature mountains behind the pilot house. At times, the captain thought his vessel seemed more like a submarine than an ore boat. Still it struggled on.

In the wheelhouse, Captain John Eisenhardt, age 31, was worried about his new command. At 1,481 gross tons, the *Noble* was relatively small, but the all-steel carrier was tough and only four years old. He had confidence in his ship, but she carried 2,900 tons of steel rails, overloading her and causing her to ride lower in the water than she should. As waves swept the main deck, she shuddered with their passing. In this terrible spring storm, Captain Eisenhardt feared for her stability.

Ahead lay Minnesota Point, a narrow eight-mile strip of land that separates Lake Superior from the safety of the harbor.

"We'll make it yet," the young captain vowed. Soon he would be able to make out the twin beacons, one on each side of the 1,000-foot concrete piers that guarded the entrance to the protected harbor within. Refuge at last — in fact, at this end of the lake, it was the only shelter.

Between cloudbursts, the skipper could see in the distance the lights of the hillside city of Duluth. Closing in fast, ahead of them in the storm and darkness, should be the entryway. This was a dangerous time; many vessels had missed the entryway, only to run up on shore; others had hit the pier, some to stagger into the harbor and sink.

"Captain, I make out a light," the helmsman cried. "There!" he said, nodding his head in the direction, his hands firm upon the struggling wheel.

Captain Eisenhardt stared: "But where's the *other* one?"

"Can't make it out, skipper!"

In mounting horror, both men peered into the raging darkness ahead of them, bearing down on the narrow entryway by their own speed and shoved by the waves. Unknown to the *Noble*, the light on the south pierhead had been put out by mountainous waves; the fog horn had also been drowned out.

"We can't go in on just a single beacon," the helmsman yelled. "We'll end up on the rocks."

The young captain pressed his face to the pilothouse window. The narrow canal pier lay ahead — but which way? He was running out of room to maneuver; waves were carrying his vessel toward a rocky shore. There was only one choice remaining: "Haul her around to port, Mister."

"Aye, sir." The helmsman began the risky turn that would place the long ship broadside to the huge breakers — the most risky point of survival in the heavy seas.

Immediately, he felt the wheel go light on him as the overloaded hull careened dangerously — the ship was in danger of broaching. The seas had the vessel in their grasp, shoving on her beam ends, the heavy waves smashing directly at her vulnerable cargo hatches.

"Get her around!" Captain Eisenhardt commanded. "We've got to face those seas."

A wave enveloped the ship, pitching her bow sharply down,

twisting her aft section out of the water. She groaned, shaking under tons of water, and shuddered. Then she was facing the storm.

"Head up the shore. We've got to get some protection from this gale."

"That's hours away, skipper! She's not handling right. I think we took on some water in the hatches when we made our turn."

The captain looked back over the spar deck. Waves were now washing over the deck, burying it under tons of water. Had the seven hatches held? Or were they letting water below?

Heading directly into the heavy seas, the ship pitched savagely. She shuddered from bow to stern as she pounded into the terrible northeaster. Her engines were on full power now, her wheel biting deep.

Time passed. Suddenly, from deep within the ship, they heard a new sound. It was the agony of the big ship's metal twisting and straining. Tons of steel cargo were shifting. She began riding lower in the forward section.

To the eyes of the captain and helmsman, the seas began to take on the towering height of five-story buildings.

Suddenly, in a single wave, a million tons of water roared toward them, obliterating the bow, then slammed into the pilot house. It shattered the forward windows in its icy fury, tore the helmsman from his wheel, and smashed into the young captain.

The *Noble* made her final voyage to the deep. She was never seen again.

On the dark shore, anxious watchers scanned the waves for the overdue ship. Some had seen the lights of a ship out on the raging lake, but they thought that the young captain and his crew had headed northward again — turning to face the raging storm in hopes of finding another port.

Another ship captain reported he had seen the lights of a vessel fighting the seas, but as he watched the lights had disappeared. Perhaps a rain or sleet squall had blotted them out, he thought, and forgot about his observation until days later, when he heard that the *Noble* was missing.

When the storm had cleared off the lake, the *Noble* was not to be found anywhere. She was missing with her captain and entire 20-man crew — their bodies have never been found. The legend of the lost ship began to grow.

Some say that the *Noble* sank after making her turn somewhere along the north shore, her savagely twisted hull and her crew imprisoned against the inland sea's restless floor. But from atop a hill overlooking the stormy lake had come reports of lights winking in the distance, moving about, disappearing for a while, then reappearing. The ship's lights, it was said, were those of the missing *Noble*.

And even today, if you listen to the legends of the lake, you will learn that some say she is still out there in the mists and can be seen on certain nights, her young captain at his first command, still in the yellowed lights of the pilot house, along with his ghostly helmsman and crew, anxiously searching for the safety of a harbor they cannot find.

It was back to reality for me, perched atop the port tube of the Zodiac. I was just getting accustomed to the bobsled-like ride when Jerry Eliason, the diver at the helm, slowed the engine to idle, then left his controls to begin fussing with the instruments set in a pod in the center of the craft. This was the gear they had used in other, successful, searches: a depthsounder, much as the fisherman had used, but with a paper printout, rather than the liquid crystal display. The printout would provide a permanent record of everything that the depthsounder located on the bottom. Also on the pod was a large compass and the all-important Loran receiver, a remarkable navigational device that could electronically "home in" on any target with an accuracy of within a few feet. Jerry had already compiled his Loran chart with grid coordinates.

We began. The Zodiac lazed along at about three knots, engine turning over at little better than trolling speed. I watched the picture being drawn of what was below us at about a hundred feet. The bottom showed clearly as the rising and falling bottom line of the continuing graph; in between, I saw, were black dots. Many large black dots.

"Just fish." Jerry seemed uninterested.

We came to the end of the Loran coordinate, turned, moved to a new heading, then slowly motored the other way.

The September day became unseasonably hot for Superior, and I wondered at the mugginess. I was perspiring heavily. As I looked toward the horizon, there was a strange darkening of the waters, and in minutes, it was upon us. The wind had switched to a northeasterly direction, and with a blast shook the open boat. The waves began to build, sending spray into the boat.

From my perch atop one of the tubes, I looked at waves coming squarely at me. Somehow, just before they rolled over the open inflatable, the boat would do a little dance, and, with a "thump" sound, rise to meet it. I moved from the weather side, and that got me out of some of the spray.

"What's that?" I partially rose, pointing to the depthsounder. A block appeared on the bottom of the depthsounder's graph. It seemed solid — rising out of the bottom below us.

"I don't know, but it interests me." Jerry turned the boat, and the graph followed. He seemed to brighten. "In fact, that's possibly the most interesting thing I've seen all day."

He reached for an anchor tied to nylon line, then tossed it overboard, wrapping the stout line around his shoulder.

"This is the high tech part," he said with a grin, then we moved off under power. "I can feel it skipping off the bottom, just barely digging in at times," he explained.

I realized what he was doing: dragging the bottom over the promising area. Presumably, if the anchor caught, he would find something. I also wondered what would happen next: would he be flipped out of the boat? He seemed nonchalant.

The wind abated somewhat as we continued the search without finding anything. What was left of the day brightened into technicolor; we had scoured, methodically and carefully, the area where the wreck was supposed to lie. The diver brought up the anchor, hand over hand.

I wondered aloud: "What could the fisherman have seen?"

"We don't know," Jerry said, shaking his head. "But whatever it was, it isn't where we searched. We had the right bearings and depth. And it couldn't have moved."

"It sounded like the real thing," I said. "The man and his wife had seen something — they even described going over the spar deck and the pilot house — with a mast sticking up."

"Well, it was one of the better reports we've gotten — sometimes people think they see things down in the water, or hear of old rumors of wrecks," Jerry said. "But it's almost impossible to search the entire area they think that it might be in. Here we had a specific report on an LCD, with specific bearings, and even a depth. And whatever was down there then, isn't down there now. I'm satisfied to that."

The waves slapped the sides of the Zodiac as Jerry leaned over to unclamp his underwater gear. Then he headed back toward the entryway, turning up the engine to a healthy snarl — and we began to plane over the water, catching the speeding waves and surfing down their fronts.

It was a wild, exhilarating ride, and all too soon we were inside the entryway and in the calm waters of the small harbor.

Jerry and Kraig shook their heads sadly. It had been a careful search, but it had yielded no results — the *Benjamin Noble*, a prize lost ship of Superior, had eluded us.

"In many ways, to look for lost ships, you really have to believe in Santa Claus," Jerry concluded.

The search was over. But the divers had shown me a paper graph from their discovery of the *Onoko*. I had been surprised when I saw the image it contained: I thought that a sunken ship would be readily identifiable by its shape, cabins, or even masts. But the 287-foot long ship had shown up on the graph paper only as a black block lying on the bottom — definitely not a rock or reef — but it didn't look like a ship either. Still, they could measure it at being nearly 300 feet long and 50 feet wide.

Jerry Eliason and Kraig Smith had found the historic vessel the previous season, near Knife River — where some said the *Noble* had come to rest. The *Onoko* had sunk in 1915 in about 200 feet of water. From navigational charts of the area, nothing was supposed to be on the bottom in that area, much less a block of those dimensions.

They made electronic passes, just as we had done, then dragged an anchor along the bottom until they could hook it to the mass. The divers went overboard and down the anchor line into the darkness, until, only a few feet ahead of them, lay the sunken ship itself. From that point on, it was a matter of searching for identifying characteristics along the hull itself and for signs of the name of the vessel — usually found fairly quickly in Superior's cold, preserving waters. They were able to make out the remains of the ship, torn in half from the stresses of sinking, as the *Onoko*. It had taken about 600 hours to locate the vessel.

I felt a little sad as I watched Kraig and Jerry deflate and fold their Zodiac. They put their boat, engine, electronics and other gear on a small trailer towed behind their automobile and prepared to return to their homes.

But I knew they would be back again — and again — to follow the leads of other sightings. Somewhere in the depths of this, the deepest, largest and coldest of the Great Lakes, was the *Noble*. And I wished them well in their quest.

Still, my mind could not leave the legend of the ghost ship.

High above in the sky, the eerie Northern Lights flashed and danced. There was an almost pinkish mist on Lake Superior, rising on the horizon like fingers. From their anchorage behind the island, a couple relaxed in the cockpit of their sailboat, watching the strange night.

Suddenly, one of them pointed toward a dark shadow in the mist.

They could hear the unmistakable thumping, thumping noise of heavy, ancient machinery, and then the splash-splash in the waters of a single, large propeller. As it emerged from the mists, they could see it was a large ship, a ghostly white bow wave in her teeth.

Was it the lost ship of Lake Superior? Probably not, but the lake plays strange tricks.

In the ghostly yellow lights of the pilot house, winking though the haze, a young captain stood beside his helmsman, looking as though he was still searching the dark shore for the port he could not find so long ago.

CHAPTER EIGHT

THE LAST
OF THE
SHEILA YEATES

It WAS A FINE SUMMER MORNING. The first monochromatic rays of light were mixing sky and sea in shades of gray. As I squinted out into the big lake, I could make out something dark and graceful on Superior's waters. The *Christian Radich*, an old-fashioned clipper-style sailing ship, was working her way with the wind. When the square-rigged Danish ship sailed majestically into the harbor, I dashed along the Duluth waterfront to get a much closer and longer look.

But I stopped short.

Another ship had caught my attention.

In front of me, bobbing gently in the harbor's waves, was a beautiful new wooden boat, all bright and shiny, with fresh paint and newly cut sails. It was the *Sheila Yeates*.

I forgot momentarily about the other ship, staring in admiration at this new boat just beginning her life on these big waters.

I could see she was built of wooden plank, on oak frame, in the old way of wooden vessels. Her bowsprit jutted jauntily, her two tall wooden masts soared sturdily toward the heavens from her planked wooden deck.

She had sailed across the Great Lakes on her way down from the boatbuilders in Lunenburg, Nova Scotia. She had been launched in 1976, just in time to sail in the Tall Ship ceremonies in New York Harbor that commemorated the nation's Bicentennial. Lake Superior was to be her home.

I stood for a while looking over her rigging and her furled sails. Her topsides gleamed in the morning sun, and I could see that this topsail ketch had character: her racy lines were patterned after a Civil War era sailing ship. Whoever her creator was had vision and obviously knew what he was doing. At 50 feet length on deck, with her bowsprit jutting out further, she was a sturdily built, ocean-going vessel that would have a good life in this great lake.

I wished her well, this new tall ship on Superior.

I learned that the *Sheila Yeates* was the dream ship of her skipper, Geoffrey Pope. Planned in the 1960s, the vessel was named for the skipper's only daughter, Sheila, combined with the name of his mother, whose maiden name was Yeates. Captain Pope had a lot of history wrapped up in his vessel; he wanted to use it to tell people about cruising Lake Superior. His crew members were people interested in Superior and in sailing the old style of wind ship. Volunteers came to spend spring weekends doing maintenance, to refurbish and refit the vessel for each sailing season.

When the skipper taught a class in coastal navigation, I immediately signed up. Captain Geoff Pope in person was then a wiry man in his 70's, modest in stature. Despite his age, he moved with the agility of a born seaman; his arms were muscular and his shoulders were broad. As a young man, Pope had been an adventurer. Back in the 1930's, he had canoed from New York City to Nome, Alaska. In the class, Pope told about coastal cruising, navigational fixes, dead reckoning, and chart plottings. But I began to gain a sense of his perspective on sailing his sturdy wooden ketch when he talked about the big lake his boat called home.

"How many of you think it's a big deal to cross Superior?" he had asked. A number of the class raised hands.

"Well it's not," he said. "It's been crossed by all kinds of vessels, including even a few centerboard boats."

He fondly recalled days on his big ketch when he and his party took down sails in the middle of the lake — and feasted on lobster and drank chilled chablis. It was a glowing picture of life aboard a big vessel.

But some tales I heard were of hardier stuff. One neophyte sailor told of timidly boarding the *Sheila Yeates* at a northern port as a storm lashed the lake. "I thought we'd stay in the harbor," he reported to me, "but we sailed right on out into it. Nothing seems to stop that boat."

Indeed, Captain Pope and the *Sheila Yeates* seemed to be in their element in a storm — rugged skipper and rugged vessel. Though Pope was not one to take what he felt were unnecessary chances with his beloved boat, a siege of weather that a neophyte might feel was stormy wouldn't trouble him. And Superior was Superior. He had grown accustomed to its ways.

"We were in rough weather, and I was at the helm," an amateur sailor related, "when all of a sudden, a wave came on board. Two crew members ahead of me on the deck began swimming. I had to hold the *Yeates* on course, but we were being shoved by the grip of that wave.

"I was having a bad time of it, when, all of a sudden, I heard the skipper yell, 'Get back on course!'"

He grinned as he finished the tale: "Captain Pope had been down below, sleeping. He had awakened only when he felt his boat moving off course."

At another time, someone had telephoned me, worried. "I've been hearing stories about that lake. I wondered if I really ought to go out on the *Yeates*."

I didn't hesitate. "She lives on that lake," I emphasized. "Take the cruise. You'll have a grand time." And he did.

More and more people crewed the green-hulled *Yeates*. I knew of teachers who helped pay for her upkeep, taking time to cruise her for a few days each summer. The crew also held fundraisers for the *Yeates*. I contributed a few of my books to be sold at a public auction.

It seemed to me that as the *Sheila Yeates* aged, her skipper, then in his late 70s, seemed to be smitten more and more by wanderlust. She dashed about Superior, crossing to and from Canadian ports. She explored little-known islands and coves on the rugged Canadian north shore.

In 1985, Captain Pope and his crew sailed from Superior across the Great Lakes and into the North Atlantic to Greenland and back.

It only whetted their taste for what was to come.

One day, a friend excitedly called to tell me that the *Yeates* was looking for paying crew members. For $60 a day, I could sign on to do a section or all of a voyage to England and back. I could cruise the Great Lakes, get off in New York, or Iceland, or go all the way to England. Or, I could fly to England and cruise back to Superior. Or do the whole trip.

It sounded like a dream voyage. A full-rigged topsail ketch, bounding through the Great Lakes — and on to England!

As it turned out, I couldn't go when the *Sheila Yeates* sailed on her first, and last, Atlantic voyage.

She left Lake Superior in May to wend her way through the Great Lakes, up the St. Lawrence River, and then out into the North Atlantic. The crew consisted of seven members, including skipper Pope. Another 40 crew members would join the *Sheila Yeates* at various points on the trip.

On July 6, the *Yeates* and her crew left St. Anthony, Newfoundland, bound for Iceland, where more crew members were scheduled to come on board. But as she approached the southernmost tip of Greenland, a point about 80 miles south of Point Farewell, she found herself surrounded by pack ice and in fog.

The ice was further south than normally expected, and the massive chunks were engulfing the wooden vessel. At 2 a.m., the *Yeates* went on the air with a radio Mayday call for help. Two fishing vessels tried to reach her, but turned back because of ice.

A Danish trawler heard her cry; the *Kiviuq* sailed blindly in the heavy fog, listening for the stricken vessel's coordinates on the radio. There were shouts from both crews as the *Kiviuq* suddenly appeared through the heavy morning fog and broke through the ice surrounding the *Yeates*.

Calling down instructions, the captain of the Danish fishing vessel got a line to the stricken *Yeates*; the crew came on board the larger vessel.

They towed the *Yeates* through the channel the Danish vessel had already cut and out through the ice. Then their course was easterly across the North Atlantic, toward Scotland. The uncrewed *Yeates* was towed about 500 feet behind the trawler. Pope was in hopes of repairing the *Yeates*, and radioed friends and crew members that he hoped to have the wooden ship repaired in about a month, after she reached port. Then she could resume her cruise.

Pope watched his vessel under tow riding well for about 400 miles until heavy weather arose. The Danish vessel's normal speed was 23 knots; but it slowed to 16, the least it could do and still keep its own schedule. The *Yeates'* hull speed was 6 to 8 knots. But even at the reduced speed, the *Yeates* was taking a terrible pounding.

Storm seas began boarding the *Yeates*, but there was nothing Pope or his crew could do. In the heavy waves, with the vessels lurching about, there was no way to keep a crew on the wooden vessel to man the pumps. She had to go her way alone and unmanned — and had to take her own chances. They stopped to examine her twice, and there was no water in the bilges.

She passed through one storm; another arose. Wave after wave battered her; then she began to ride lower in the water.

They examined her a third time — and now there was water in the bilge. Was she leaking from her battering in the ice field? Had some of her seams loosened or a plank come unfastened?

No one knew. Worse, there was nothing anyone could do.

Finally, with a heart-wrenching finality, the wooden boat had to be cut free.

It did not take long. She grew heavy by the bow, and as she sank beneath the waves, the bow ripped off. Then, lofting her stern to the skies, she slipped beneath the North Atlantic in about 4,200 feet of water.

The *Sheila Yeates* was 13 years old. Captain Pope was desolate at the loss. "It's the end of the line for the *Sheila Yeates*," he told reporters. "At my age, I don't think I'll be able to find the money to build another boat."

Several years later, I talked with Captain Pope again. He seemed almost timeless at age 80, with his white hair and beard. Topsail ketches were still a great love of his life, and at one time, I knew he had hoped to build a ship to replace the *Yeates*. He told me the cost of a new boat would be close to $800,000. "What do you do when you don't have that much?" he asked, but did not expect an answer.

I nodded sympathetically, but I knew. You don't build a new ship, but you keep up with your love of the sea.

In fact, he had just returned from an attempt to navigate the Northwest Passage, a 3,000-mile journey from northern Greenland westward to the Bering Straits between Alaska and Siberia — an icy passage that had already killed many sailors. Pope had signed on as a crew member on the 57-foot fiberglass Bowman ketch, *Cloud Nine*, skippered by Roger Swanson. *Cloud Nine* had sailed up from St. Thomas, in the U.S. Virgin Islands, and pushed 2,000 miles into the passage before ice forced it to turn back — the only U.S. flag private sailing boat ever to get to Resolute — and then ended his voyage five months and 8,000 miles later in Falmouth, England.

Moreover, on board *Cloud Nine*, Captain Pope had rounded Cape Horn, had been in the ice of the Antarctic, and had even gone on to circumnavigate the world.

His beloved ship was gone, but the captain had not stopped sailing.

CHAPTER NINE

AN HOMAGE
TO TWO WRECKS

I FOUND THE BONES OF THE ANCIENT NAVY sloop of war almost by accident years ago. It was a bright, sunny day as I jogged along the long sand spit known as the Minnesota Point, just out of downtown Duluth. The Point, separating the Duluth and Superior harbor from Lake Superior, is the world's largest freshwater sand bar, and was a grand place to be for a struggling young writer just out of the U.S. Army.

Each day I drove my ancient car across the Duluth aerial lift bridge into downtown Duluth, where I worked for the Davidson Publishing Company; nights I returned to a tiny wooden house far out on the Point, located directly behind a sand dune. It was from neighbors that I first heard the story of an old Navy ship that was sunk somewhere in the waters along this sandy beach.

"They burned her for the copper," I was told. Salvagers were at work one winter when the wreck washed further ashore and the water froze over. They put the torch to the old ship so that they could more easily wrench out her copper keelbolts and other fittings. It seemed like a waste of a shipwreck to me.

My search ended nearly at the end of the Point, about a third of a mile northwest of the Superior, Wisconsin, ship canal. There it was, lying black against the bright sand beach: the almost unrecognizable bones of an old ship. I could not make out much, only large pieces of dark wood that jutted from the water. As I drew nearer, I saw what looked like a ship's keel lying in the clear waters, with remnants of ribs sticking up.

I held my breath for a moment as I waded out, but I was lucky today. The Point had been blessed by a calm offshore wind and had been kissed by days of golden sunshine. The shallow sand beach had done its work, for the usually chill water was luke-warm.

The wreck was in shallow water. Putting on my diving mask and snorkel, I lay down in the water to peer at the old wood timbers. The front part of the wreck was almost on the beach, and the old vessel extended out in the gently sloping water, until, at the end, it was covered by about four feet of water.

I floated motionless in the water, gazing downward, fascinated. What a sight! Though blackened, these were still sturdy remnants of a large wind ship. I had the immediate impression that this was a powerfully built vessel and that the builders knew what they were doing.

Something gleamed. Swimming closer, I saw it was a copper bolt, lying underneath part of the heavy wood structure. I wondered what it was for: something that held part of the old vessel's inner structure together? It was about an inch thick in diameter, and about a foot long, fitted with what looked like several washers at one end. The end was thicker than the washers, and it appeared to have been pounded over. I later learned that this was a drift bolt, with cinch rings.

I marveled at the old wreck that one could walk up to on this wonderful beach. I was also curious what her story was, and why she was left to rot here.

Searching for information, I found that around these last bones was woven a tale of history that stirred the blood. She was the U.S.S. Essex, built over a hundred years ago, an ocean-going Naval ship which had ranged the world. What was more, she was one of the last vessels built by Donald McKay, the American master builder of clipper ships that set so many ocean-going records for sailing.

Today, the *Essex* is believed to be all that is left of McKay's fabulous ships, and as such is an archeological treasure — an irreplaceable part of history. The irony is that the once-proud sloop of war had not died in battle, but had been deliberately burned, sunk and left to rot in the shallow waters near Duluth.

McKay was America's foremost shipbuilder. His name became synonymous with his world-ranging clipper ships which set many records in the great days of sail. McKay's ships seized and held the imagination of sailors everywhere with their beauty, grace and speed.

As a boy, I spent countless hours building a model of the most famous clipper of them all, *Flying Cloud*, which in 1854 set the world's record of 89 days 8 hours around Cape Horn from New York to San Francisco — a record broken only in recent years by a modern racing sailboat. The hundred-year and more record of McKay's ship is all the more impressive when one notes that the clipper was fully loaded with passengers and cargo.

McKay's other clippers, now irretrievably lost along with the *Flying Cloud*, bore names that ring with romance and adventure: *Sea Witch, Sovereign of the Seas, Lightning* and *Stag Hound*. All set records for long-distance speed that were unequalled in their time — over 400 miles in a day — and flew under acres of canvas on masts more than two hundred feet tall. One of McKay's clippers, the *Champion of the Seas*, achieved a single day's run of 465 miles, a record that has never been broken for a cargo-carrying vessel under sail.

Legends in their day when sail was in its greatest glory, McKay's clippers were once called the finest example of a sailing ship, a unique combination of beauty and speed. With their clouds of white canvas on seemingly slender spars, they caught the world's attention and imagination. McKay's clippers had the ability to race around the world faster than ever thought possible for a sailing vessel. Never before or since the glory days of the clipper ship, have wooden vessels been so heavily rigged, overcanvassed, or driven so hard as were the American clippers. The *Flying Cloud* was noted for her speed in storms.

None of McKay's vessels outlived him, except the *Essex*, lying here off the Minnesota Point, and the *Glory of the Seas*, which spent her last years in Puget Sound as a floating fish storage plant, then was towed ashore in 1923 near Seattle and burned for her copper metals and other fastenings.

From the last bones of the last-surviving McKay ship, I could only get an idea of the story that the *Essex* represented. She was history, a cousin to *Flying Cloud* from the same master's hands. As I touched her timbers, I could only use my imagination to catch fleeting glimpses of the fine old ship. How she must have appeared, years ago, her decks awash, her tall spires and rigging groaning in the storms; white cloud of sails slamming her hull through the world's wild seas.

As I gathered more information, I learned that her construction had been authorized by President Abraham Lincoln, just prior to his assassination. She was part of the *Enterprise* class of vessel, delayed because of financial difficulties after the Civil War. For ten years, no major new U.S. vessels had been under construction, but now the *Essex* would be one of eight that helped represent a young United States to the world.

She was a naval "sloop of war," a three-masted sailing machine but with a 1,200 horsepower steam-powered auxiliary engine turning a single screw. She was commissioned on October 3, 1876. At 185 feet in length, she was a relatively small vessel — the *Flying Cloud* was larger. Displacing 1,375 tons, the *Essex* had a 35-foot beam and drew 14 feet, three inches. As an *Enterprise* class vessel, she carried as her main armament four smooth-bored 9 inch guns, one 11 inch gun, and one 5-inch gun, which was a Parrott rifled muzzle loader. Like other vessels of her day, the barque-rigged, wooden hulled warship carried a full suit of sails and relied largely on her sail power for ocean voyaging.

From pictures and drawings of her, I could see that she was an impressive vessel. This was not a slab-sided navy warship, with boxy lines, but a windship, made to slip easily through the water. She had a sweet, gently curving sheer; the McKay heritage was unmistakable in the jut of her clipper-type bow, long bowsprit and fine entry. Tall masts ranged skyward from her wooden deck, and, aside from a tall, black smoke funnel between and fore and mainmast, she looked like a sailing ship from the days of America's great square riggers. Under steam, when her sails were furled, she carried the U.S. flag on a special staff in her jib boom.

One of the last sail-powered fighting ships built of wood for the U.S. Navy, the *Essex* ranged the world, visiting many important ports. Regarded as one of the finest ships of the fleet, she was first assigned to the North Atlantic, then later, the South Atlantic Squadron. She cruised to Liberia and along the west coast of Africa. From 1881 to 1882, she sailed the Pacific and in 1883, she became part of the Asiatic Squadron. During this assignment, she afforded protection to missionaries at Ponape, Caroline Islands, during a native uprising. She was in Manila Bay in Cuba when the *U.S.S. Main* was sunk; she was sent on a relief mission when Admiral Perry discovered the North Pole.

After about 27 years of service, she left her salt water environment to sail the Great Lakes, first in Ohio where she served for 12 years more in the naval reserves. By 1917, she was berthed in Duluth, Minnesota, and sailed to Chicago to serve at the Great Lakes Training Center. By this time, she was a very old ship and her maintenance was sparse. One of her tall masts had been taken down, the spars largely removed, and she moved on her steam power alone. After World War I, she was stationed at the Minnesota Naval Reserve docks, located on the inner side of Duluth's Minnesota Point.

In 1927, the once-proud square rigger was stripped of her engines. An ugly wooden structure in the form of a large shed was built atop her deck so that she became a floating naval reserve office ship in Superior harbor. She was taken off the Navy list in 1930.

The *Essex* had earned a special distinction by this time: she was the *last* McKay vessel, having outlived all the other ships of her famous maker. She was also the oldest steam-powered vessel in the navy and its last wooden-hulled sloop of war.

She was sold for $410. On October 31, 1931, the 55-year-old *Essex* was ignominiously towed out of Superior harbor to Minnesota Point's lake side. There the last McKay vessel anywhere in the world was lashed with a steel cable around each side and doused with 200 gallons of kerosene and oil, and set on fire.

An eyewitness account in the *Evening Telegram*, Superior, Wisconsin, reported on her fiery death:

"Most of the good oaken ship *USS Essex*, once one of the finest vessels in the United States fleet, was being scattered over Lake Superior Thursday in the form of charred bits of wood. There were no ceremonies to mark the *Essex's* end. Even the American flag, ever conspicuous during her naval and naval militia days, was lacking. The burning of the grand old ship of the line was supervised by the United States government, which gave orders that nothing be left in the lake to menace navigation."

She blazed through the day and the night. After she burned nearly to the waterline, the salvagers hooked up steel cables and she was winched groaning onto the beach. Salvagers tore through her blackened bones for copper and bronze spikes and bolts.

Over the years, what was left of the *Essex* remained in Superior's shallow waters, pounded by surf and encrusted by ice. From time to time, amateur salvagers and souvenir seekers came across her partially beached bones and used chainsaws, hacksaws, prybars and axes to get more driftpins and bolts — or just to get firewood for a beach party.

In 1992, the remains of the *Essex* came under the scrutiny of archaeologists hired by the Minnesota Historical Society's newly funded State Historic Preservation Office (SHPO). They officially surveyed the remains of the wreck, which then consisted of a 50-foot length of the hull's bottom, with portions of the keelson, portions of the frames, and a few hull planks still remaining. At the time of the survey, the wreck was partially submerged, extending out from the beach into approximately four feet of water. The wreck shifts in position from year to year, and some years it lies underwater and is difficult to locate.

But enough was left to nominate the *Essex* to the National Register of Historic Places. Scott Anfinson, of SHPO, who worked on the early efforts on behalf of the *Essex*, said that the nomination was justified because the wreck can still be used to document construction methods on mid-19th century naval vessels. The fact that the vessel was designed and built by Donald McKay, he emphasized, makes it all the more significant. The *U.S.S. Essex's* wreck was placed on the National Register on April 14, 1994.

Anfinsson feels strongly about preserving the *Essex*. "It's an artifact of history like no other in Minnesota," he said. "She is our only naval vessel and may be the last surviving example of Donald McKay's genius still in American waters. Go and touch a piece of his work — you can't do that any place else."

He emphasized, "Naval archaeologists say you can still see the master work in the wood. This was a person who knew wooden ships."

"When I go there," he said, "I always feel a sense of wonder that these few fragments speak to me. I can visualize the complete vessel with its tall masts, yards and arms. Every time I talk about it I get choked up. Something abut the *Essex* gets to me."

And it does to me, also.

The *Essex* is the most historic vessel on Superior, but there was another special sunken ship that interested me.

"She's out there, you know," Dave Nixon, the chartermaster, told me one day. "I flew over her and you can see her on the bottom."

I knew of her only by reputation, but I knew she was huge — well over 300 feet in length.

"Bigger than a football field," Nixon said. "A northeaster got her."

What the chartermaster and I were interested in was a sailing vessel that lies in the Apostle Islands group, northeast of Outer Island, in a little over 50 feet of water. This was the wreck of the *Pretoria*, one of the most colossal wooden vessels ever to have sailed Superior. At the time of her construction, in 1900, she was one of the largest wooden boats ever built, not only in the Great Lakes, but possibly the world. Her bones attest to her colossal size: 338.4 feet in length with a 44-foot beam.

"The *Pretoria* is an impressive ship — a big beast," says underwater archeologist David J. Cooper, who has been on the wreck many times. "We're old friends," he said, adding: "She truly is bigger than a football field, and in wood. On a clear day, you can see a long way down the hull and get a good feeling for her size."

Though equipped with three masts, complete with sails, the *Pretoria* relied upon a steamer for towing. A schooner-barge, the *Pretoria* criss-crossed Lake Superior often, with her maiden home port Duluth.

She came to a violent end after five years of service. On September 1, 1905, the *Pretoria* loaded a cargo of iron ore at the Allouez docks in Superior, Wisconsin, for a routine run to Chicago. Despite storm warnings raised by the U.S. Weather Bureau, the *Pretoria* put to sea in the tow of her consort, the 263-foot Davidson-built wooden steamer, *Venezuela*, also carrying a cargo of ore.

By evening, the captains knew that this was not to be another inconvenient fall storm, but a true killer gale — in fact, it was the deadly 1905 storm that broke up the steel steamer *Sevona* on the Apostles' Sand Island Reef. Winds howled at more than 40 miles per hour, and high waves battered the *Pretoria*.

About 30 miles northeast of Outer Island, her steering gear broke. The *Pretoria's* Captain Charles Smart signalled the *Venezuela* of his ship's dire problem, and the tow desperately tried to alter the *Pretoria's* course back into the shelter of the Apostle Islands.

But the towline snapped. As the *Venezuela* attempted to come about, she lost sight of the powerless schooner barge in the rough seas and darkness. The *Venezuela* searched for the *Pretoria*, but ultimately sought shelter and returned to Ashland, reporting her loss.

Despite the storm, many veteran sailors were not overly concerned about the dangers facing the *Pretoria*. She was strongly built, they reasoned, as well as new and very large.

Alone on the lake, the *Pretoria's* captain ordered her sails raised on the 100-foot high masts, but these quickly blew apart. Because she could not steer, the schooner-barge wallowed helplessly in the rough seas.

The northeaster, in fact, was so severe that it shoved the fully laden *Pretoria* sideways across the lake at an estimated rate of between three to four miles an hour. This pounding put heavy stresses on her hull in a way she was never designed to absorb.

Huge waves smashed into her bulwarks, slammed across her deck into the cabins, and shoved against her hatches. In the height of the storm, her steam pumps gave out, and in the stress of the wind and waves, the giant vessel was slowly being torn apart.

Captain Smart ordered the ship's anchor to be dropped, but it did not catch until about 2:30 p.m. when the ship neared Outer Island. She came to anchor less than a mile to the northeast of Outer Island, within view of the Outer Island lighthouse.

Lighthouse keeper John Irvine reported on Sept. 2: "A terrible gale blowing from the NE. The biggest sea I have ever seen since I have been at the station, which is eight years."

At anchor, the *Pretoria*, hammered by the northeaster, slowly began to come apart. The captain reported storm waters slashing through the hatch coamings, forcing some hatches off. Under relentless pounding, the covering board gave way; waves tore off sections of the decking. It was all over for the ship: Captain Smart and his nine-member crew lowered their lifeboat to head for shore.

Lighthouse keeper Irvine reported he saw the small boat leaving at 4 p.m., and he hurried down to the beach with a white flag in his hand and a piece of rope to render "what assistance I could." But as Captain Smart and his crew neared the surf-pounded shore, their lifeboat capsized, throwing the men ten feet into the air. Irvine helped save the captain, mate and three seamen as they washed ashore, hanging onto their overturned boat. Four seamen and a cook drowned.

The *Pretoria* settled on the bottom in 52 feet of water, her masts protruding above the raging seas.

The next day, the steamer *Venezuela* searched for her lost escort. The lighthouse signaled the steamer's crew, who sent a boat ashore and took the survivors off. As a final note, the lighthouse keeper wrote, "I expect she will be a total wreck as her decks is all coming ashore."

She was later salvaged, with her iron ore cargo taken from

her hold. A salvor recovered the steam pump and one of the *Pretoria's* masts. Divers located and recovered her anchors, each weighing 3,500 pounds, and donated them to the historical museum on Madeline Island.

Sections of her anchor chain, also salvaged, are part of a chain fence in Bayfield. A further section can be seen on a statue, which includes a part of the *Pretoria's* boiler, at the water's edge by the main docks.

Though a wreck, the *Pretoria* is of interest to underwater archaeologists, like McKay's lost sloop of war, because of her colossal size and her sophisticated construction. Her strong timbers came not from East Coast shipbuilders, but from Michigan; though lesser known, she is one of the final, and perhaps the most accessible, surviving example of Great Lakes builder James Davidson's great vessels. She is an important ship for archeological, architectural and historical information, and even today, maverick Great Lakes shipbuilder Davidson is held in respect for successfully pushing the size limits on wooden ships.

In the *Pretoria*, he had built one of the world's finest and largest wooden cargo vessels.

For perspective, one needs to realize that in 1898, when the *Pretoria's* keel was laid, eastern maritime circles felt that Great Lakes shipbuilding was inferior to that on the Atlantic and Pacific seaboards. Critics argued that the Great Lakes vessels lacked the supposed staunchness of ocean schooners, and suffered in design and construction.

Today, underwater archaeologists have lifted the myth and found that the *Pretoria*, and others like her, were actually technically superior in many aspects to coastal built, ocean-going vessels.

David J. Cooper and John O. Jensen, of the State Underwater Archeology Program, Division of Historic Preservation at the State Historical Society of Wisconsin, wrote in their book, *Davidson's Goliaths*, that the *Pretoria* compared favorably with another giant of her day, the *Wyoming*, built in Bath, Maine.

The *Wyoming* was launched in 1909 and was the last and the largest wooden six-master ever built, at 329 feet. Yet the *Pretoria* was even larger, at 338 feet. Beamier and deeper in draft, the

Wyoming's 3,730 gross tonnage was nearly a thousand tons more than the Pretoria's 2,790 tons.

The more costly *Wyoming* had a capacity of 6,000 tons, as opposed to the *Pretoria's* 5,100 tons, but in an all-important analysis of the two vessels, the *Pretoria* carried significantly more cargo relative to the gross dimensions of the two vessels. In their analysis, Cooper and Jensen point out that the *Pretoria* had 1.83 tons capacity per gross ton, as opposed to the *Wyoming's* 1.61.

The two underwater archaeologists also analyzed problems of size in a wooden vessel. Though the *Wyoming's* builders relied on traditional wooden shipbuilding methods, with massive keelsons up to six or seven feet high, the big schooners ran into problems in rough weather, leaking badly with their hulls twisting with a snake-like quality. Though they were supposed to operate in the North Atlantic, the continual working of their hulls made them heavily reliant on their pumps.

As they grew older, the hulls increasingly loosened — and builders of the six masters began to talk openly that they were too long for wooden construction. All eleven of the six-masted Eastern-built vessels came to a violent end.

Unlike the Maine builders, Great Lakes builder James Davidson had broken with traditional schooner designs to successfully go beyond the 300-foot length. His main construction innovation was to integrate pieces of steel into a wooden hull structure, adding strength with little loss of cargo capacity.

The *Pretoria* was loaded with Davidson's strengthening techniques: steel plates reinforced its wooden keelson and its hull was strapped with steel diagonals between frames. The *Pretoria* also had steel cross bracing, steel trusses and iron arches. It also had an iron band around the inside of its wooden hull, which gave it great strength and staunchness.

The fact that Davidson was able to build massive wooden ships into the 20th century, when nearly all other builders had gone to steel, marks him as an exceptional, if not a well-known builder. His vessels — the final phase in the development of the Great Lakes schooner-barge — were eminently successful on the Great Lakes.

Most lived to an old age and were abandoned during the

Great Depression. Some were deliberately sunk, rather than salvaged. *Pretoria* met a violent end.

In their analysis, Cooper and Jensen pointed out that Davidson's schooner barges and steamers, operated in tandem, offered cargo capacities comparable to the steel ships of the turn of the century and could be built for much less cost. In one comparison, the *Venezuela* and her consort barge, *Pretoria*, had a combined capacity of nearly 8,000 tons and represented an investment of around $200,000. By contrast, the *Rensselaer*, a Cleveland-built 474-foot steel bulk carrier, carried only 7,500 tons and cost nearly twice as much — an estimated $350,000.

The *Pretoria* is today a popular SCUBA diving site, and, unlike predatory early divers, modern underwater sportspeople hold conservation-minded attitudes, taking nothing back to the surface but photographs. It is also illegal these days to take anything from a wreck in Superior waters.

There is an epilogue to the lives of the shipbuilders and their great ships that lie under Superior's waters. Donald McKay, who found fame with his great clippers and his wide-ranging sloop of war, the *Essex*, died in relative poverty on a farm in Massachusetts.

In contrast, by the time he died in 1929, Great Lakes shipbuilder James Davidson had amassed a fortune. He left shipbuilding when the Great Depression closed his yards, but went on to other investments in shipping companies, shipyards, and banks. In his shipbuilding years, he left a legacy which brought Great Lakes wooden vessel architecture to one of its highest peaks of technical achievement. The *Pretoria* remains an underwater monument to his genius.

So they are gone, all of Davidson's ships — and all of McKay's. Not one American clipper ship, sloop of war, or Great Lakes schooner barge, has survived afloat.

CHAPTER TEN

RAINY DAY
IN PORT

RAIN DROPS THRUMMED on *Persistence's* wooden cabin top, just inches above my head. I gently lifted the forward hatch above my berth to peer out. Sheets of rain off in the distance made the lake, and the day, appear gray. It was not that I hadn't sailed before in wet weather, it was just that, given a choice, I preferred not to. Sometimes on Superior I did not have that choice.

No question about it: today was a rain day in port. I wouldn't be sailing today.

Drops of rain splashed me and I gingerly let the hatch fall shut and sat back, reflectively. Rain sometimes made me feel good, like today, for then I could sit in my comfortable bunk, relax and think. I was alone, and at times, that could be very good.

I was reminded of the old Solo Sailor's poem:

I am the captain of my craft,
My word is law from forward to aft.

I am the cook and bottle washer, too;
I am also the passengers and crew.
And though it's said I'm hard to please,
At least I'm not afraid of mutinies.
In fact, my crew at sea
Is just about as perfect as it can be!

Perfect or not, the only thing the crew had to do this morning was to begin the day with my ritual cafe latte. The ship's galley was close. In fact, all the crew was obliged to do was slide over to the starboard side of the centerboard where I found my fist-sized espresso maker and my self-lighting butane stove. I could handle my coffee chores from my bunk, as I often did. A few spoons of coffee, a cup or so of fresh water, and in a few minutes, there was a burble and a splash — and the first drops of dark, brown coffee began running into my metal cup. The stove was also nicely warming my small cabin.

A sip of latte and my mood was mellow. It was a splendid day to be inside a wooden ship, going nowhere, just sitting and rocking. Though I could hear the rain thumping down above me, I was warm and comfortable.

My mind moved easily over memories of some of the people I had met on this special lake. Some are adventurous, often kind and wise, and many of them shared special moments and insights with me. I sat back to think about them and this wonder that is the world's largest inland sea. It was a good day for reminiscing and remembering.

I was in the pilothouse of the motor vessel *Wenonah*, plowing through lumpy seas and thick fog on one of the last voyages of the season to Isle Royale. Because of its remoteness, the isolated 210-square mile island off the Minnesota shore is the north woods primeval, one of the last unspoiled domains for wolves and moose. The ancient Indians came here to mine copper so pure it startled the world. The bones of many ships lie near its rugged reefs. And for a while, a tiny Norwegian fishing village clung tenaciously to its tip.

The old Captain, Stan Sivertson, was at the wheel to guide the *Wenonah* into Isle Royale's Washington Harbor. We were close, but I knew from checking the radar that we had to shave past a rocky headland in the fog.

"Look outside now," he told me. "Maybe you'll see something. We're in the channel now."

I peered through the pilot house windows, but I could see nothing. The world was silver, enshrouded in fog. Water blended with mist.

"We've got to ease our way in," the old captain said calmly. "We need to get past a sunken wreck and squeeze by the other channel. See anything yet?"

I opened the pilot house door and walked cautiously to the railing. I felt the fog on my face; it misted my glasses.

"Up high," he suggested, and I almost jumped back. Nearly on top of us, looming out of the fog, was a pine tree.

"Close!" I muttered respectfully as the old captain steered the *Wenonah* past the tree and through the narrow, rocky passage. I saw he had a merry twinkle in his eye. He had guided his boat through the narrow pass countless times. And probably he had startled many passengers just like me on days like this.

Later, as he swung his vessel to show me the south part of the island where he was grew up in a tiny Norwegian community, he told me about the sunken boat we had just passed over. He sighed nostalgically, remembering his happy boyhood life on the island, but one pitch black night, he was called out of bed. As if in a nightmare, he heard his father yelling, "The *America* is sinking, the *America* is sinking."

With his brother in a small boat, he rowed toward the harbor. At first sight, he recalled thinking that nothing was wrong. The *America's* bow was up against the reef, and when he was a quarter of a mile away, he told his brother, "It's just sitting there." Then he saw the boat capsize.

"I saw the skylights over the engines and all the windows in the passenger staterooms blow out, just like geysers, when she rolled over and went down. I was so shocked at the sight of her sinking that this was the last thing I could ever remember of that night."

He shook his head. As we headed further into the fog, he reminisced about what it was like to be a youthful fisherman on Lake Superior.

He went out in a 20-foot open fishing boat, and on windy

days, spray came over the side; some days as he baited hooks he could see icicles forming on his fingernails.

"It was pretty cold with bare hands," he said, adding "if you had a big breaker, sometimes you could get them on board and they could swamp you."

He'd seen a lot of Superior's storms, too, but the one he particularly recalled was in June, 1964, just after he'd bought the *Wenonah* in Chicago and was bringing her to Lake Superior. As he entered the lake from the Soo locks, the wind was blowing from the southwest. Captain Sivertson recalled that one of the crew members told him, "Oh, it's going to be a beautiful night on Lake Superior."

"We got past Whitefish Point and I started steering for Isle Royale at about 10 p.m., and it was just beautiful, absolutely calm with no wind at all," the old captain said. "I went down for a little sleep, but at about 2 a.m., I woke up wondering what was happening to the boat. My gosh, it was jumping up and down, pounding hard. At about daylight all we could do was head straight into the northwesterly wind because we didn't want any breakers over the side, or to catch us on the quarter, to take any more pounding than we were getting. We had already idled down so that we could just barely steer against the wind. I realized we were out in a real bad one."

"Suddenly, we could see this one big wave coming at us, maybe two miles away, running above all the other breakers. In the sunlight it was almost eerie, it was so bright. I wondered if we could go around it, but then I realized I couldn't turn: we'd catch the sea on the side and that would give us an awful walloping. So we kept on going, and then this wave would disappear behind other breakers, three or four minutes, then appear again.

"Finally it hit and then I was holding onto the wheel, going downhill just as though I had jumped off a cliff. We had gone down into this hole in the water, and suddenly, the wave just filled her up again, burying the bow. Finally she came up, shaking the water off. We kept on going, despite the weather. When we got into Isle Royale that night it was dead calm again."

In later years, I called him occasionally; sometimes I visited him on his boat. He had the distinction of being the last man to fish commercially off Isle Royale, now a national park. Even in his mature years, he worked six days a week, often getting to work at his fishery at 7:30 a.m.

"If I had to retire to the land somewhere, I'd go daft," he told me. "I fear the lake in a storm. It's a very awesome force. But I have to be by it. It's my life."

Captain Sivertson died in 1994 at the age of eighty, just days short of his eighty-first birthday. Though he had had heart surgery the previous year, Captain Sivertson was back at work in his warehouse in Superior, Wisconsin, sorting through his fishing gear, getting his nets and his boat ready for a fishing trip to Isle Royale.

That night at his home in Duluth, the old captain suddenly collapsed after suffering a stroke. His last words to his wife were: *"Don't call 911."*

Other memories flooded in. On a voyage back from Isle Royale, I was in the *Wenonah's* wheelhouse, looking out at the spectral fog as we seemed to glide along on calmed seas.

The *Wenonah's* first mate came over to stand beside me; it was obvious he felt like talking. The grayness of the day seemed to be affecting him also.

"My brother-in-law got killed out here in a storm one night," he announced. "In his canoe."

"Why would anyone want to be out on Superior in a canoe?" I asked. "In a storm?"

He shook his head. "That's what I asked when my sister called me. I couldn't figure it out at the time, either."

"I was living in Grand Marais, Minnesota, and I had gone to bed at about 10:30 p.m., when my sister called to say that her husband had gone out on the lake. And all she could think of to say, when I asked her why he went out, was to answer, 'What do you think? The wind is up.'"

"She was obviously in a state of shock, and when I asked her, she said she'd called the Coast Guard and she told me they wouldn't go out. I called some friends of mine, but of course, there wasn't much anyone could do if the Coast Guard wouldn't go out. We decided we'd have to wait."

The next day there were 15-foot waves on the lake that would splatter "like a spray gun" when they hit the North Shore. He and his party searched up and down the shore for a distance of about eight miles, in case the missing canoeist was able somehow to make it back. The Coast Guard sent up a plane and about 2:30 in the afternoon, they called to say that they had found him.

He began to speak slower, and in a low voice: "The way we figure it, his 16-foot aluminum canoe had been blown off the beach that night and he went out to get it. He had been watching television, and had just slipped on his boots, but didn't have winter liners or socks or gloves. He took another canoe out, but the wind had come over the tree tops, howling down on the lake about 200 yards from shore. I figure that when he transferred from the one canoe to his canoe, something must have gone wrong. He lost the first canoe— and we found that four days later about eight miles down the beach.

"When they finally found him, he was three miles south of his house about 15 miles out in the lake. He was right in the center of his canoe, just huddled up. The Coast Guard said they couldn't understand how he could even be afloat, because there were still 12 to 15-foot seas. But he had centered himself perfectly in his canoe and he had stayed afloat, despite wind and seas. There was nothing he could do. He had no paddles and no motor."

"That was how they found him," the First Mate concluded sadly, "Still upright, but frozen solid — and dead."

Not all my Isle Royale memories were as grim. One of my favorite movies is *Never Cry Wolf*, based on the Farley Mowat book, and that reminded me of a time when I was on Isle Royale and talked to a ranger who told me about his arrival on the island for a winter study.

It was a grim February day; the temperature was 23 degrees below zero and he had flown in on a ski plane — the same kind that was in the movie.

"The plane clatters, bangs in on the ice," he said. And he had stood on the ice and watched his plane take off, leaving him with a stack of baggage sitting on the ice. "It looked like it did for that poor fellow in the movie, isolated in the middle of nowhere."

He added, "You remember in the movie where the hero's hair seems to stand up on the back of his neck?"

I remembered the memorable scene: The hero is stranded alone on the ice and looks around, but there is nothing; the eternity of the ice, winter and the utter wilderness, sinks in. "What happened to you?" I asked.

"I walked off the ice to the bunkhouse and put my feet up before the fire. You see, there were several naturalists that had been here before I arrived."

He had been invited to see a wolf kill. Later, in a plane, he and other rangers flew toward the south shore of the island, where wolves had slain a moose. He continued, "But there was another moose standing off to one side of the kill, and within 20 yards, five or six wolves lounging around. The moose was just standing there."

"I'd have thought that under those circumstances the moose would be running away."

"Well," he explained, "probably you had danger when you had two moose. But one of the moose was killed, so that took away the danger to the other one. The wolves had what they were looking for."

That was one of the balances of nature, for the island is a living laboratory for the gray wolf and the moose in the wild. The wolves probably came out in one pack from the Minnesota mainland on the ice, and over a period of time, grew into three or four packs, numbering as many as 40 wolves at one time. Now, as a threatened and endangered species, wolves have their largest single concentration in the continental United States on Isle Royale.

The thought of all those wolves around startled me. With campers on the island, as well as myself walking about in the woods, I had a few questions about co-existing with the carnivores. I had never been this close to wolves before.

The ranger shrugged his shoulders. "From the standpoint of the wolf as predator against man — the old medieval, hungry, salivating killer wolf type of thing," he said, "I don't know if you'll find them ever threatening man. They're an interesting animal, but humans have done a job of eliminating them because of prejudices or historical inaccuracies."

I looked around at the deep woods surrounding the ranger

station. Wolves were here on this island, and, though these days most campers are reasonably enlightened, I wondered if anyone here had felt threatened by a wolf.

"Anybody I've talked to that has seen a wolf on the island has never felt threatened by them. More than anything, they just caught a fleeting glance anyway," he said.

"Actually, they're a little like people," he continued. "Wolves have their families, they have their ways of going about getting their food, and they have their family structures. They're an interesting animal."

Had the ranger ever felt threatened by a wolf?

"Never even seen one!" he replied.

I looked out over the harbor. Soon it would be fall and I wondered how long the ranger stayed on his wilderness island before he had to leave for the season. He told me he waited until late in the fall for a final sweep of the island to be certain it was "all battened down for the winter."

Then he added, respectfully, "There's always the question of getting off. We just sit and wait for that good day, about the first of November. Fog is no problem, for radar can conquer fog. But if you get a six to eight foot sea rolling, you've got problems. We've got a 26-foot Bertram here and in the spring, it took me 2 hours to come over in that; but going back last year it took 5 1/2 hours on the lake. I felt like a bottle in the ocean."

I had another sip of latte, and my eyes alighted on the skin-diving mask, flippers, and snorkel I carry on board. The underwater gear reminded me of a man I met in a SCUBA diving shop in Thunder Bay, Ontario, after I had sailed *Persistence* up from the Minnesota North Shore.

He was a slim, wiry-tough man wearing well-faded jeans and a knit shirt top; his arms rippled with muscles. He moved with some care, for he was just out of the hospital after a diving accident. I judged him to be in his early thirties, and he told me he had been a commercial diver on Lake Superior for nearly fifteen years.

I told him about my interest in SCUBA, and we began chatting. I wondered what it was like to be a professional diver.

"One of the notions that a lot of people have," he said, permitting himself a wry grin, "is that they're going to dive down and find some treasure ships. You hear this all the time. And they think they'll become a commercial diver and make a million dollars right off the bat and everyone's going to want them, and there's going to be clear water and they can walk into a bar and say, 'I'm a commercial diver,' and the ladies are going to jump all over them."

"But what actually happens," he said, "is that you learn how to build bumpers, swim underwater, and take pictures and look at fish."

He explained, "When you become a commercial diver, you go into the water because something's wrong. Ninety percent of your work is in zero visibility and strong currents; it's cold, dangerous and hard. You work your butt off."

"And, er, the ladies you mentioned....?" I was enjoying his tale.

"If you say you're a diver, they're probably going to go the other way."

This was a different picture of diving life than I had imagined. At least no one had yet explained it to me this way. "If the water is dark where you dive, how do you see?" I asked.

"You don't. You do it by feel."

The typical diving job, he explained, is pipefitting. "You lay pipelines. Make joints, weld, and cut them." He elaborated that divers also work with explosives and do photography. They also lay in concrete forms and work with jackhammers. "When I go to work," he explained, "I put on my suit, my helmet and a pair of coveralls, I have a crescent wrench in one hand and sledge hammer in the other, and they drape a cutting torch over my shoulder."

His hard-hat diving gear included a 70-pound weight belt and a 35-pound helmet. When I asked why he didn't use SCUBA, he said it was because the tanks have a limited air supply.

"If you get caught on the bottom, you're in trouble," he added. Another problem with SCUBA gear, he pointed out, is that the regulator requires more effort to use than a hard hat. "If you're really working hard and sucking on that regulator, SCUBA drains more energy out of you than when you just turn the air on in the hard hat and you have an atmosphere of air around your head. The pressure is easier to breath and you don't have to schuss....schuss," he demonstrated. "With SCUBA, every inhale you have to force; every exhale you have to force," he said. "And even though it's very minor, after two hours on the bottom it can tire you out."

"The longest dive I've spent around here has been three and a half hours," he said. "In the Great Lakes, the typical dive is around 30 to 50 feet. At 50 feet you can stay quite a while; at 30 feet you can stay as long as you want. I've done a few dives to 140 or 150 feet; these come about once or twice a year. Around here we've doing a little bit of salvage on a wreck someplace, pipeline stuff; we don't have any reason for deeper dives."

He grew reflective. "Lake Superior can be beautiful and serene at times," he said. "Minutes later, you just know you're looking at death. That's why you find it infinitely challenging. You never relax on that lake. I think it's more dangerous than the North Sea."

I glanced out the portlight. It was still raining, but out there in the mists, I knew, was another historic island. I had been on Madeline Island many times, but today my reminiscences went back to the summer of 1984 when I took my first lengthy voyage in my little boat; Madeline Island had been my first stop.

I became fascinated with the island's history that went back to the earliest days of exploration of the lake. It has been under three flags, French, British, and United States, and many of the old-time voyageurs settled on its wooded shores during its fur trading heyday. The first "black robes" had been here, too, gathering their flocks. Madeline also has the distinction of being the only island inhabited year-round on Superior.

One day, in the company of the Old Commodore, Bill Peet, I found myself in a car on a rutty trail leading into a patch of dark pine woods on the east side of the island. We had to stop part way because of the bogs of water and branches.

"He probably keeps it this way on purpose," the Old Commodore had snorted. "He can get in, but few other people are willing to try."

We left the car on the trail to walk the rest of the way through the heavy woods, then came upon a sun-drenched grassy knoll overlooking the lake. Perched atop it was a two-story house with many windows and a large shed. Inside was the man we had come to see, Rufus C. Jefferson.

With his shirtsleeves rolled up over his elbows, Jefferson looked every inch an ex-Navy man with his close-cropped steel gray hair and ramrod-stiff bearing. He was at work on a new 28-foot wooden sailboat, which he designed and was building himself. He was about to clench-nail a plank to a steamed oak frame.

"Can I help?" I volunteered. This would be a new experience for me — working on a traditional wooden boat. I picked up a heavy hammer and placed its head on the steam-bent frame as he hammered a clench nail through the plank. In three strokes, the heavy nail came through the frame and struck my hammer, its tip folding over. The plank and frame were now clenched together by the nail, the old-fashioned, and very strong, way to fasten a wooden boat.

Soon we were talking about boats, Lake Superior and even old clipper ships. He had just returned from the Falkland Islands, where he had helped survey some of the old clipper ships that had been there for eons, for the Falklands had become a graveyard of the last of the great sailing ships.

He also gave me some tips on solo sailing, including the advice to trail a long line after my boat. That way, if you fell overboard, you could grab onto it, he said, adding: "Twice I fell overboard, and the only thing that saved me was that line. I grabbed it and pulled myself back on board. Otherwise, I just would have watched my boat sail off without me."

He went back to work on his wooden boat, and, as we walked off, I inquired of the Old Commodore: "Tell me if it's true that he only goes sailing when it storms."

"Oh, it's probably true," the Old Commodore said, shrugging his shoulders. "You know, that's when it's the most fun."

"How about during a northeaster?"

"He claims he gets bored and he 'heaves to,' so the boat can steer itself slowly, then he goes below for a nap." He indulged himself a wry grin. "He must get a lot of sleep."

He continued, "Let me tell you about Rufus and our first Madeline Island to Isle Royale race. Rufus doesn't want anything to do with being called a yachtsman, so officially he wasn't entered in our race. But there he was, anyway, at the starting line. He claimed he was just going out 'cruising' in the same direction of the race.

"Well, he didn't fool anybody. As the race neared Rock of Ages reef on Isle Royale, Rufus's little sailboat was one of the first boats there. But Lake Superior got to be Lake Superior, and when we got back to Madeline, there was no sign of Rufus."

"I got worried, so I hired an airplane to look for him or the wreckage of his boat. Eventually, my search circle extended far enough that I found him on the other side of the lake. There he was, he and his little boat, just sailing along. And when I finally talked to him on the radio, he had the audacity to claim he had finished cruising and just wanted to do a little real sailing." He harruped dramatically to emphasize the point.

Rufus's death came as a shock to me. One day, several years ago, I heard a report that Rufus had gone missing; to get more information, I called one of the islanders, Nori Newago. She told me that a northeaster had sprung up suddenly when Rufus was sailing, and that an extensive search had been made, but neither Rufus nor his little boat have ever been found.

Back on board *Persistence*, a gust of wind struck the mast, and the boat shivered a bit. As I glanced once again out the portlight, my memories flew back to another man on this lake who had a role in Superior's greatest mystery. There were others involved, too, but they no longer had a voice, for they had been the victims of a tragedy.

It was a blustery, dark day as Captain Cedric Woodard entered Superior from the Soo Locks from the east, upbound for the Port of Duluth. Captain Woodard was the ship's pilot on board the Swedish freighter, *Avafors*, and turned to advise the tough Swedish captain beside him on the bridge: "We sure as hell have got no business out here."

The salt-water captain could barely hold back his contempt: "Pilot," he snorted, "It's only the lakes."

The barometer dropped steadily as the storm cell intensified, then roared directly over Superior. As the afternoon grew long, the wind screamed, blowing half of the wave tops right off.

The *Avafors* was taking a terrible pounding. The sea she was heading into was not just big rollers, but practically straight walls of water. The waves were slamming the ship so hard people could barely stand on their feet; Captain Woodard worried that his kneecaps would break.

In eight hours, the *Avafors* had managed to travel only an estimated 12 miles into the head seas. For two hours, she had not gained a ship's length. Her radar had gone out after two especially big pounders.

When the pilot house door was ripped off, the tough Swedish captain turned to Captain Woodard and said, "We've got no business out here."

But by that time, Captain Woodard knew it was too late. There was no turning back.

That fateful November day, another ship was out there, to the west of the *Avafors*, and having a bad time of it. At about 5 p.m., winds were gusting to 96 miles an hour, with some wave heights at over 30 feet. Captain Woodard answered a mysterious radio call.

"Who in the hell am I talking to?" he finally snapped, not recognizing the voice nor all it was saying so urgently.

The strained voice responded, "The captain."

Captain Woodard apologized. "It didn't sound like you," he finally said to Captain McSorley, of the 729-foot ore carrier, the *Edmund Fitzgerald*.

At about 5:30 p.m., Captain McSorley made radio contact again. "We are taking heavy seas over our decks. It's the worst sea I've ever been in."

That was one of the last calls that the doomed captain of the *Fitzgerald* ever made. As the *Avafors* kept radar track of the *Fitzgerald*, now trying to make the shelter behind Whitefish Point, a snow squall descended. Superior was at her worst.

By 7:25 p.m., when radar beams again swept the seas, where once steamed the *Fitzgerald*, there was nothing. The 729-foot ore boat had simply disappeared — she did not even have time to radio a final Mayday.

The *Avafors* made port later; Captain Woodard took part in the official Coast Guard investigation and hearing on the sinking, with the loss of all hands, of the *Edmund Fitzgerald*. He played an important role, for he was one of the two men who talked directly to the doomed ore carrier that fateful day in 1975. He shared some of his insights with me; I remember talking with him several times about his experiences on the lake that November day and learning his thoughts on the missing ore carrier.

Now he, too, is gone from this lake. In 1975, the year the *Fitzgerald* sank, he retired as a Captain and as a Great Lakes Pilot. He died April 9, 1995, the year of the 20th anniversary of the *Fitzgerald's* sinking.

Now evening came pleasantly. This had been a special day on the big lake for me, spending time remembering old friends, acquaintances, and recalling stories and memories. I felt rewarded.

Later that night, as I rolled back into my sleeping bag, I was grateful for this rainy interlude. It had let me rest and gather energy for what lay ahead.

What I planned to do next was sail all the way across the lake.

PART THREE

STORM
CROSSING

"Would'st thou," the sailor questioned,

"Learn the secrets of the sea?"

"Only those who brave its dangers," came the answer,

"Can comprehend its mystery."

CHAPTER ELEVEN

RACING
THE STORM

BY THE TIME I CLAMBERED on deck to have a look around the Port Superior harbor, I could almost feel trouble ahead. There was a dampness to the morning that a weak and intermittent sun could not cure. I squinted into the distance and saw that, past the breakwater, mist clung heavily to the water, turning Lake Superior a shade of light gray.

My little boat rocked in the harbor swells despite the fact that there was no wind; I felt a certain heaviness to the air. I had a sense that things would probably get worse before they got better, if I was any judge of this lake.

Superior, I knew, was not a lady to be trifled with.

"What's the forecast?" I hollered at charter master Dave Nixon, as he strode along the bulkhead. Dave would know; Dave always knew.

"Not good," he said. He paused momentarily to shake his head. "A low is heading our way."

Lows mean storms on Superior — not a time when a sailor

wants to be out in a small boat of any kind, if it can be avoided. Right now, I was snug enough in my own wooden boat alongside the bulkhead in front of the Port Superior office. I looked about, checking my sloop: I had tied her with three-eighths inch line fore and aft, and I had five fenders overboard.

Thom Burns, one of the veteran sailors I'd be voyaging with, walked hurriedly along the water's edge. He'd be the ship's navigator.

"What do you think?" I called. "Are we going?"

He peered at me through his glasses, his shoulders shrugging his uncertainty. "Joe has to make up his mind," he answered.

Joe Boland was the owner of the *Tullamore Dew*, the boat in which we'd be traversing the lake. Yesterday, I had been on board the powerful 35-foot sea-going catamaran, helping prepare the boat for our crossing from the Apostle Islands area to the bottom of the lake and through the locks to the "Soo" — Sault Ste. Marie, Ontario, Canada.

Joe was not encouraging. "The latest weather forecast says that the low is stalled right now," he said. "That means it could take off and hit us at any time."

I rummaged about my boat, a little relieved we weren't heading off right away. It was prudent to wait to see what the storm would do: would it lie off the headlands, giving us clear passage, or would we get out into Superior's open waters — only to be hit hard?

I'd been in Lake Superior storms in my own boat, so the decision not to rush into the long voyage did not exactly distress me. Superior could be a violent, treacherous body of water. Besides, I was starting to feel sleepy; I had not slept well the night before, waking in the early morning hours with worries about our trans-Superior voyage. Now I settled down in the cabin, thinking of a catnap.

Suddenly, Bruce Boland, Joe's son and our fourth crew member, stuck his head into the hatch. "We're going!" he announced, his face wreathed in a grin. Then he left.

Despite the oncoming storm?

I hurriedly glanced at my watch. We were late getting started — it was almost 10 a.m. Would we get caught in the storm? Or have to sail through the night?

This was supposed to be a pleasure cruise, I grumped to myself. I hurriedly hauled out my sailing gear, locked my boat's hatch, then dashed out the dock to the waiting catamaran.

Joe explained as we got underway. "We've got to be at the head of the lake by Wednesday," he said. "Besides, there's a Great Lakes Cruising Club rendezvous, and if we don't get there in time we will have a difficult time finding a good slip."

"What about the storm?" I asked.

"We're going to try to outrun it!"

Joe fired up the two diesels, one in each hull, and moments later we cast off the lines. White water kicked up as *Tullamore Dew* backed out of her slip at the end of the pier, then headed out past the breakwater's green-winking light.

I took over the helm, steering the course dictated by the navigator. The big cat cut easily through the bay and soon I felt the water beneath the twin hulls change as we came into the open lake. There was a light swell running from the north and east. The wheel felt cool to my touch, and the lake was chill, even in July. A gray mist covered the lake.

I steered alone in the cockpit, while down below, Joe, Thom, and Bruce huddled over the charts. These were seasoned sailors: I was happy to be in their company and, now underway, relieved at last to be on our voyage. Joe was a veteran Great Lakes sailor and owner of the cat; Thom was editor of *Northern Breezes* sailing magazine and a former Navy man. The youngest of the crew, Bruce, had many years of Great Lakes sailing experience.

The twin 27-horsepower diesels purred healthily beneath me at about 2,800 r.p.m.'s; I checked my knotmeter: the cat was moving at 6.8 knots. I was becoming familiar with the feel of the boat and its latest Global Positioning System (GPS) instrumentation. By pressing several buttons, I could call up navigational information, such as course heading, speed and distance. All of this came from satellites orbiting the earth about 22,000 miles away. I compared my knotmeter and helm compass with the GPS information, but they seemed to be at odds with each other by several degrees.

When navigator Thom Burns sauntered on deck, I pointed

out the differences of several degrees of heading and different knotmeter speeds, sometimes as much as several tenths of a knot. "Think of the GPS as a slow computer," he suggested. "It's presenting you recent history; the compass and knotmeter are giving you real-time information."

He looked over the wide transom at the wake shining in the gray waters. It curved first to one side, then the other, before it disappeared into the mist. I saw what he was looking at. A wave train slapped the forward port hull, tossing it easily a few degrees to one side, and as I corrected my steering to keep the boat going straight, I sometimes did not correct enough, or corrected too much. The result was the snake-like wake behind us. I discovered steering in a straight line was not easy.

The mist turned to rain when Thom took the helm. I put on my foul-weather gear, and went back to the open cockpit. Despite the fact that it was July, and that back home everyone was probably roasting in summer heat, the lake had a tomb-like chill that was getting to me. I had added a sweater, but when I took over the helm again, I started to shiver in the rain.

We sailed on. South of us lay the rugged Porcupine Mountains — and little else. The shoreline was rugged and inhospitable; the Porcupines themselves came steeply down to the water's edge. Here were some of the tallest mountains in the Midwest, with elevations up to 1,200 feet. There had been, miles back, Black River Harbor, a small harbor where we could have ducked in for the night. Ahead lay Ontonagan, the only other port in a lonely coastline. Otherwise, if a storm arose, there was no other protection for us.

Our shipboard barometer had been dropping steadily — an ominous sign that the storm was coming close. The weather channel had also issued small craft warnings.

At a strategy meeting, we considered getting off the lake and staying overnight at Ontonagon Harbor, but this was nixed by our navigator. "If the storm arrives as expected from the north to northeast quadrant, we'll be pinned on the south shore for days by 10-foot waves," Thom emphasized.

After all, we were winning our race with the onrushing storm. Our calculations called for us to be inside the protection of the breakwaters of the Keweenaw Waterway before the storm was scheduled to arrive over our section of the lake. The forecast called for it to hit sometime early in the morning, at about 1:30 a.m. or so. We'd come to the breakwaters, and gain the protection of the inland waterway, at about 12:30 and we'd be secure at our harbor about halfway up the waterway by 4 a.m.

So it would be an all-night run for us on Superior.

The race against the storm, now in deadly earnest, was on.

Night quickly enveloped us. Alone at the helm, I looked about me: it seemed as if the world ended with the boat. Below, the water moved darkly, but I had lost my sense of direction and motion. Ahead of me on the bow, a white running light gleamed into the fog, but I could see little further than that in the dark. We were running nearly blind in this dark sea; I hoped sincerely we did not come across another boat, or find some object floating in the water. I watched the digital readout on the compass rise, then kicked the rudder to port to correct several degrees. The big cat came quickly back to course, the twin rudders biting deep in the cold waters.

I was concentrating on my steering, alone in my murky world of fog and darkness. Somewhere ahead of me lay the Keweenaw Entryway, our exit off the lake. But if I approached the stone entryway as much as one or two degrees off course, I'd run up on shore. Or possibly even hit the stone wall itself. My responsibility as helmsman was to get us in, right on the nose. I knew that below, inside the cabin, the skipper and the navigator were following my progress on their navigation gear as we approached the dark shore.

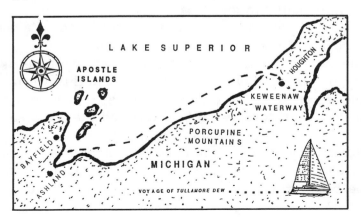

From time to time, I turned my face to the direction I thought the storm might come from. I could almost feel the chill of the low approaching us. I huddled beneath my foul-weather gear, my glasses misted up, both hands on the steering wheel.

I got some protection from the canvas dodger that covered the forward section of the cockpit and the hatch, but that also presented a problem for me. At well over six feet in height, Joe Boland could easily look over the dodger, but I could only peer over its edges. I solved that problem by stepping up on a sturdy ice chest that we kept in the cockpit. Then I could peer over the dodger while hanging onto the wheel to try to see something in the onrushing dark. The visibility in the fog was only about 50 feet or so. Not much comfort for the helmsman.

There was a ghostly feel to the sky and water now. The horizon looked the same in every direction; the fog obscured everything that lay beyond the ship. The fog reflected back the light of the masthead and the bow running lights, giving off a spectral glow. I was getting tired: the previous sleepless night was catching up with me. Staring into the fog did not help.

I shook my head as if to clear it, determined to concentrate on steering; it was easy to lose a few degrees of course in these rolling seas as my mind drifted in and out of its own thoughts. I turned the wheel and watched the digital numbers march up on the compass, and, seconds later, on the GPS. I had given up steering by the GPS display alone; in these swells, it was just too slow. Now I read the compass, and checked it with the GPS. I was holding the boat on course for the Keweenaw, now only hours away.

"We'll make it yet," I thought to myself. Down below, the crew were huddled over the main cabin table, playing cards.

Suddenly, there was a low, moaning sound that came closer and closer. With a shriek, it descended; I could feel the sailboat caught in a great rushing of wind.

Tullamore Dew threw her bows to one side, then began a slide at an angle, her deck canting as if one bow was on an elevator. I spun the wheel hard to starboard, but there was no stopping her.

I had lost control.

With a gut-lurching crash, we plunged the port bow into a wave trough, then lifted off again, bursting out of the storm wave. I spun the wheel some more; suddenly, she lurched upward for a moment, then righted herself.

"What was that?" From below, in the cabin, came shouts. Someone threw open the hatch.

"It must have been a microburst from the approaching front," I said. "I couldn't hold her when that first gust came through. But she seems steady now."

It was a short-lived example of the ferocity of the weather system. It threw the big cat about as if it were a toy — but only for a short period.

I glanced at my watch. We had received our first knock at about 11 p.m., and it would clearly be a long night ahead. We'd just had a taste; when the real storm arrived, it would be a major blow.

I peered into the darkness; it wasn't the size of the waves that made my heart pound, it was the speed with which they roared. One bow would be hit by a wave train, causing a shudder, then the wave would pass underneath, dipping the bow, only to repeat the whole motion across the second bow.

We pounded along, up, down, and sideways, as if on a watery elevator without a sense of direction.

The fog descended heavily about us, cutting our visibility in the storm. We were flying along, almost blind, headed for a big stone entryway somewhere ahead in the dark. I knew that the entry, with massive stone piers jutting out into Superior, had claimed its share of shipwrecks.

I glanced below and saw Thom concentrating on his charts and his GPS navigation equipment. We'd have to get in very close to see the entryway's piers.

Joe came up to take over the helm as I moved forward in the cockpit, peering out into the fog. Somewhere, I knew, there was the north breakwall extending out into Superior, with a lighthouse that was supposed to be flashing a white light. We should be able to see it on a clear night for miles at sea. There was also supposed to be a fog horn; and, on the south breakwall, another light.

From the navigation station below came Thom's voice. "Well,

we're here," he said. I could detect an undercurrent of worry.

"*Where?*" Joe wanted to know. And so did I.

"The GPS says we're just off the pier," Thom emphasized. "It's right ahead of us."

Beyond the bows, I could see only fog and blackness. My stomach did a quick lurch.

What lay ahead? If we went in too close, we might end up on shore or smash up against a breakwater and go for a swim. Our situation was dangerous.

Still, we couldn't stay here all night.

I peered desperately ahead, but I could see only fog. Minutes passed as the skipper began a slow circle.

I saw something off the starboard bow. Odd, I thought; my first impression was that it was nothing, but as I waited a few seconds, there it was again: a lightening, ever so slight, in the fog bank.

"Over there," I yelled to Joe, pointing. "A light."

"That's it!" he said, adjusting his course as the cat lurched forward in the swells.

Out of the fog loomed an awesome stone pier.

"Which one?" Joe yelled, worried. If the pier ahead of us was the south one, we'd end up on shore. Only going around the north lighthouse would give us safe entry to the canal.

"North pier," I said.

"South pier," someone else guessed.

"North — south — *which one!*" Joe was frustrated. He throttled the diesels back and began creeping carefully forward.

The fog lifted for a moment, revealing the light to be the north pier. To starboard was the south breakwater, but it had no light on it that I could see. Nor had there been a fog horn.

Joe lined up *Tullamore Dew* for the entrance, edging the diesels up a notch.

Inside the breakwater, the air felt like the inside of a tomb. The waterway was pitch black and filled with fog — not lighted. We couldn't remain here, even if we wanted to. The Keweenaw Waterway was heavily used by big ships; at any time, a saltwater freighter or big ore boat could come rumbling through this limited space.

Joe had the big cat barely moving. I leaned out the port side of the cockpit, trying to get a look at what lay ahead.

Bruce grabbed a flashlight and made his way to the bow pulpit, where he shone the beam ahead and to the sides. I was surprised at the narrowness of the entry at this point; it felt as if I could almost lean over and touch the heavily wooded bank with one hand. I could make out the sinister shape of shallow waters. The black waterway would be tricky.

Suddenly, I saw a light. A navigation signal of some sort, I presumed. We steered toward it carefully.

"Wait!" Bruce yelled, then waved his arms quickly, signalling a turn. "It's a yard light. From a farm."

Joe veered the cat off, and we were back in the channel, trying to steer from buoy to buoy. Our problem was being unable to see the buoys in the darkness and the fog until we practically ran into them.

Thom, who was entering all the GPS waypoints for the twenty three or so course changes, would give Joe the proper course. Joe proceeded slowly at 1.5 to 2.0 knots, using the depth meter to stay in the channel, while Bruce and I attempted to find buoys and daymarks. The channel seemed to widen.

We motored slowly through the night until we saw the first pink flushes on the horizon: morning was coming. Ahead lay the lift bridge that linked the twin cities of Hancock and Houghton. Thom called ahead on the radio, and the bridge answered almost immediately, asking our clearance height.

"Fifty feet," Thom replied into the mike.

"Come ahead," the bridge responded. We idled forward, waiting for the bridge to open. The rumble of the largest lift bridge in the world filled our ears.

To the north, on the Houghton side, was the Portage Lake Marina, just a short way past the vertical lift bridge. I looked ahead, and sighed gratefully: Yes, there was a slip open. We carefully brought the cat in to rest.

I glanced at my watch: it was 4:30 a.m.

The long night had ended. We were off Superior.

CHAPTER TWELVE

IN THE
WATERWAY

IT WAS THE SUNSHINE streaming in through the portlights, and something else, that finally woke me. I sat up and rubbed my eyes, not all that much refreshed after only a few hours of sleep.

Slowly I oriented myself. I was in my sleeping bag in the main cabin of the catamaran, gently rocking in the marina in the waterway. To the west of us was the giant lift bridge and across the water were the city docks at Houghton. We had gotten off Superior's fog in the early part of the storm to enter the Keweenaw Waterway, about halfway up the thumb of rock-ribbed Michigan land that juts into Lake Superior. We had been lucky last night.

I rubbed my eyes and fumbled around for my eyeglasses, then checked my watch and groaned. It was only about 9 a.m., and here I was. I had the faint perception that after all our adventures last evening and early this morning, that something else was about to cap our experiences. Maybe even something of a humorous nature.

What seemed liked hundreds of flies buzzed about over my head in the main cabin, with some of the more curious ones alighting on me.

I was a prime target. They were big flies that seemed intent on having revenge on these intruders in their waterway. I got up, alternately scratching and attempting to swat flies.

The fly swatter, or my aim, wasn't very good this morning. Thom entered the main cabin, scratching. I gathered that his berth in the port hull had been invaded, too.

"Catching anything?" he asked as I flailed about.

I shook my head. They were quick, these waterway flies.

Thom headed for the galley, then rummaged about. I wondered what he was doing until he held up a plastic cup, filled it about half full of water, and then added some dish-washing soap.

"Let me show you *my* fly catcher," he said with a sly grin.

Holding his hand over the cup top, he shook it a few times, then glanced about the cabin: the ceiling was filled with flies, some buzzing about, some clinging upside down.

"Here's how it works," he said, placing the cup against the ceiling, over a fly.

I watched, bemused.

"And, here you are!" He pulled the cup away from the ceiling. I peered inside the cup and saw the fly struggling in the foam.

"It works!"

"You bet," he said. Then moving quickly, he went about the cabin, jamming the cup against the ceiling, trapping the flies. He had obviously had a lot of practice. I tried the system; I had to be quick to get the cup over the fly, but once in, it was curtains for the fly.

"Works best when they're still sluggish," Thom explained. "You cover them and then they jump backwards into the foam. That's it for them."

The fly problem in the cabin resolved, I walked up to the open cockpit, then did a 360-degree scan in the brilliant sunlight. The weather had changed overnight: This was a beautiful morning in the waterway. The early mists had burned away, and the sun shone bright, though the wind was blowing a raucous 30 knots plus, right out of the north.

We were resting up for the push ahead through the other half of the waterway, then out and across more big water. The interlude was all right with me; I could use a little rest after being up all night during a stormy crossing with the added drama of fog and trying to find the entryway through the breakwaters.

Besides, as I looked about the shore, I remembered that this was a particularly interesting area. The Keweenaw Peninsula is a unique finger of rocky land that juts far into Superior and is famous for, among other things, its lake effect, which makes it one of the snowiest places in the nation. "This place was made to catch snow," a resident told me. As I gazed over the water at Hancock, I tried to imagine it snowbound in the Big Snow of 1978-79, when snow piled up Copper Country's annual average of 235 inches by January and then kept right on coming. "It snowed 40 days and 40 nights," a man told me, "and if it had been rain we'd have been building arks."

By the time the snowfall had finished, the Keweenaw had received 390.6 inches in one winter (a total snowfall of more than 32 feet.) Some people had to carve tunnels through the snowbanks to get to their homes; others coped by using portable wooden sidewalks erected above the snow.

Weather aside, I had also caught a hint of the Keweenaw's spectacular history. As dawn had lightened the waterway this morning, I glanced up from the cockpit to the high hills to see abandoned and rusty giant metal skeletons — remnants of once famous mines built during a giant mining craze, just a few years before the California gold rush.

To think that at one time this area was considered worthless. That was back in the early 1880's, when the region was considered so hopeless a wilderness that lower Michigan had to be forced to take the Upper Peninsula. Under the terms of a complicated settlement, the state received this big tract of wilderness jutting out into Superior, albeit very reluctantly. At the time the area was just another unexplored hunk of real estate in the middle of nowhere and not really worth anything.

Still, there had been rumors. It had been known for centuries that this wilderness had mineral deposits of an odd nature. The earliest explorers brought back chunks of solid copper; the Jesuits wrote about it in their journals. Douglass Houghton, a young Detroit physician turned self-promoted geologist, was the first to make a survey of the area. When he returned to civilization in 1841, he told an amazing story: He had extracted two tons of ore from a single explosive blast. From this he had picked out many lumps of native copper, including one of "about 40 pounds in weight."

The copper craze was on. Across Superior came boatloads of surveyors, miners and fortune hunters hoping to get their slice of the riches. Rumor had it that there were giant copper boulders and copper nuggets one could pick up off the beach — almost pure copper, of a grade never before seen in this country. Claims for small patches of land could be filed easily; anyone could make a fortune.

In 1842, at the mouth of the Ontonagon River, miners had found a boulder of native copper that weighed 3,708 pounds. The copper rush, following the first big strike in 1844, was bigger than the California gold rush, years later. Soon this area, once thought to be worthless, produced nearly 90 percent of the nation's supply of copper. Big mines crowned the hills of the rugged Keweenaw, burrowing deep for the main lodes. In 1916, at their peak, the mines produced 166 million pounds.

After that, the supply of the good copper was largely exhausted; by the end of World War II, the mines produced only 43 million pounds, which was 3.6 percent of total U.S. production. Prices plummeted; mines closed.

Today, deserted equipment sits rusting atop silent mine shafts. The man who started it all, surveyor Douglass Houghton, didn't benefit from the mining boom he set off. In 1845, on the western side of the Keweenaw, he was out in a birch bark canoe, continuing his surveys. A sudden storm came up on Superior and he drowned near Eagle River. His body was found about a year later.

As I sat in the cockpit, my mind turned back to last night's adventure on Superior. We had been lucky, but some boats had not been so fortunate on their run to the Keweenaw.

I was reminded of one boat whose bones we had sailed across

Building his boat, the author cut and assembled the boat's wooden frames and stringers atop a strongback, which later was removed. Persistence's *overall length is twenty feet.*

The first of three layers of one-eighth inch thick wood veneer strips (above) is stapled and epoxy glued to the stringers. Right, Loris tries out the strong construction. Persistence *took seven years to build.*

Marlin Bree stands on top of Persistence *during testing. The small centerboard sailboat will be loaded with sleeping bags, sails, gasoline, clothing, food, water, and all the equipment and supplies necessary for the author to be to be self-sufficient while on Lake Superior.*

Persistence *is loaded on its trailer and being towed behind the author's Sidekick sports utility vehicle. The mast is secured atop the sailboat's cabin.*

Right, next to a grassy bank, Persistence *lies in a slip in Cornucopia's harbor. Loris removes the sail cover and helps get the boat ready for the author's departure.*

The Apostle Island's' Sand Island Lighthouse with park service volunteer Nancy Peterson.

Above left, Persistence *is tied up at the end of the dock of Sand Island. Above right, the sailboat floats in almost gin-clear waters above the island's golden sand bottom.*

Right, Marlin and Loris relax after their walk to the Sand Island lighthouse.

Proud figurehead scanning the waves, the 76-foot Viking ship replica Hjemkomst *began a voyage on Lake Superior that ended in a special homecoming in Norway.*

The helmsman (left) maneuvers the boat with a steering ore. During storms, waves sometimes came over the stern.

The famous sloop of war, the U.S.S. Essex (1874-1931) in better times. She ranged the world's oceans in her prime, but died a fiery death in Lake Superior off Minnesota Point when salvagers burned her to the waterline for her scrap metal. What remains may be the last remnant anywhere of the work of the most famous clipper ship builder of all time, Donald McKay of Boston. The Essex was one of his last vessels.

Under spinnaker, Tullamore Dew surged ahead on a fine sailing day on Lake Superior. Off the bow is the sloop, Katy, which the catamaran soon passed. Both were enroute to the Canadian side of Sault Ste. Marie.

At rest after an overnight passage on Superior, *Tullamore Dew* rocks gently at the docks of Portage Lake Marina on the Keweenaw Waterway.

Cruising through the Keweenaw Waterway, Thom Burns (left) pilots the cat past old mining buildings. Joe Boland (right) scans the horizon along the Shipwreck Coast.

Fighting through the surf (right),
the Life Savers from the Grand Marais,
Michigan, station row hard to get
their wooden surf boat past
the breakers. The boat's captain
steers with a long oar. In storms such
as this, capsizes are not uncommon,
even for the skilled Life Saving crew.

Left, the Portage Station Life Savers
under the command of Captain Albert Ocha
on the snow-covered beach near Marquette,
Michigan. They pose after rescuing the crew of the
Robert Wallace, (background) wrecked in a
blinding late-November 1886 northeaster.

A northeaster kicks up square rollers on Lake Superior. In the background is the north lighthouse guarding Duluth's canal entryway. The steep and fast-moving freshwater waves pack tremendous force .

yesterday — the three-masted schooner *Lucerne,* lying sunken in the waters along Long Island, just east of the Apostle Islands. The 195-foot schooner had also passed through the channel between Madeline Island and Long Island. She was on the same route we had followed, eastward toward the Soo.

According to the *Marine Record,* she departed Ashland, Wisconsin, the evening of November 15, 1886, under full sail in "beautiful" weather, with the barometer "high and steady."

Though it was late in the season, her master, Captain George Lloyd, had confidence in his big schooner. He was a sailing man, in the era of the last great sailing vessels, and perhaps bitterly resentful of the encroachment of steamships. He declared he'd rather "go out with her under canvas than in the tow of any steamer."

As the giant centerboard schooner cleared Chequamegon Bay, Captain Lloyd didn't hesitate to drive his loaded vessel onward into the open waters of Lake Superior. She was carrying only 1,256 tons of iron ore, which was 124 tons short of her usual summer load, probably in anticipation of rough autumn weather. The *Lucerne* was bound for Cleveland, Ohio; Captain Lloyd intended to sail, as we did, to Sault Ste. Marie, where she would rejoin her tow, the steamer *Raleigh.*

Captain Lloyd's ship had been fitted out with new sails and fittings; the *Lucerne* was one of the staunchest schooners on the lake, sturdily built, and had a reputation for being fast. Her dimensions rated her as a large schooner at 194.9 feet in length, 33.7 feet in beam, 13.85 feet in depth of hold, and drawing about 8 feet (centerboard up) and about 16 to 18 feet (centerboard down). Built in Tonawanda, New York, and launched April 23, 1873, the 727.9 gross ton schooner carried a great cloud of canvas set on three high masts. She and her nine-man crew were on the last run of the season.

But as dawn broke, the lake erupted in the worst northeaster in years. She was heading in an easterly direction, up the rugged Upper Michigan coastline. The winds howled in her path, building huge seas along the lee shore. Though Captain Lloyd and his crew did not know it, this was the beginning of a blinding snowstorm that would sweep Superior for days.

Around 4 p.m., the big schooner was seen by the steam barge

Fred Kelley, off Ontonagon, Michigan. The vessel was taking waves over the port bow that were scouring the deck and punishing the ship. All of her sails were up, except the fore gaff topsail, and she was beating hard against the headwinds and waves.

About dark, Captain Lloyd made the only choice he could. His ship was taking a terrible pounding. With any luck, he'd be able to return to the Apostle Islands channel and tuck in behind the protection of Long Island in Chequamegon Bay, about 60 miles away. She was seen by the *Fred Kelly* turning about in heavy snow squalls and gale force winds.

Three days later, on the frigid morning of Nov. 19, the light-house keeper on the tip of Long Island was witness to a dreadful sight. From his tower, between storm gusts, he saw a vessel's ice-coated masts sticking out of the churning water.

As he fought his way along the beach, he saw what appeared to be three ice-clad figures aloft — all that remained of the *Lucerne's* nine-man crew. They had climbed the masts to escape their sinking vessel, lashed themselves in the rigging, and had frozen solid.

The bodies, chopped out days later by volunteers from Bayfield, were covered with up to six inches of ice. One seaman wore five overcoats in addition to heavy underwear, but his feet were bare. Another was also heavily dressed, but had on rubber boots. The third was scantily dressed, but had on high topped boots.

No one knew what had happened to the remainder of her crew during those last fateful hours. It was speculated that some members were swept out into the raging lake, after the vessel went aground close; others may have been entombed as she sank. One partially decomposed body that washed up on shore about a year later was thought to be part of the ill-fated *Lucerne's* crew.

The wreck marked the end of an exceptional ship in one of the worst schooner tragedies on Lake Superior, and raised a number of questions: Why did the huge schooner sink so close to shore in relatively shallow water? Why didn't she drive on through the entryway between Long Island and Madeline Island, into the protection of Chequamegon Bay? Why didn't the crew attempt to get to the beach, only hundreds of yards away? The *Marine Record*, referring to her as "literally a ship of death," had not fully explained her fate as it examined the tragedy's circumstances:

"She was found one mile from the lighthouse, and the fact that she was lying stern on, with her stem in seventeen feet of water, heading to the southeast, showed that she had not foundered because she had cast anchor close to land, and swung around in one of the most severe snow storms that ever descended upon northwest lakes. She simply pounded to pieces there on the beach, and the terrible weather rendered the crew perfectly helpless. The continuous washing of the icy seas effectually prevented the men from getting ashore. The sailors who took to the rigging probably tried to escape the seas, but they only succeeded in running into the jaws of death in another shape than drowning. They were frozen to death. No man could have lived in the rigging on such an arctic night as the one which settled the fate of the *Lucerne*."

Years passed. Onto Lake Superior came a new breed of archeologist, skilled in modern underwater archeological reconstruction. David J. Cooper, State Underwater Archeologist, Division of Historic Preservation for the State Historical Society of Wisconsin, and his dive team spent many hours surveying, measuring, and photographing the *Lucerne*. "The *Lucerne* and I are old friends," he told me and began providing new insights into the big schooner's final hours.

"There's no doubt she met gale force winds and heavy snow squalls," Cooper said, pointing out that she got as far up the Michigan coast as Ontonogan, where she was seen with sails set before she turned to run for shelter.

He added, "It's also believed that she was largely manned by a pick-up crew from Washburn, with boys eager for a sailing adventure. Though the *Lucerne* had been reinforced for her work, it was interesting to note, also, that this was her first season on Lake Superior."

It also turned out to be her last. Some people blamed her loss on the fact that she was under sail, rather than under steamer tow, but Cooper does not agree that sail power alone led to her tragedy. Cooper noted that the *Lucerne* was originally built as a grain clipper for the lucrative Chicago to Buffalo run, a virtual grain clipper race. The first grain clipper into port got the best cargo prices. As a result, he said, the ships were built big and fast and driven hard by their competitive crews.

"It was possible that 'clipper fever' was still in Captain Lloyd," Cooper theorized, "for he had served all his life under sail and as a sail master had a fierce pride in sail. Maybe he wanted to blow out of Ashland ahead of the steamer — just to show her what sailing vessels could do."

The *Lucerne's* wreck lies about 2 miles from the Chequamegon point entryway, and about 1 1/3 miles from the point light. She had been that close to the channel — and apparent safety.

Cooper theorizes that probably Captain Lloyd realized he was getting close, but because of ice and snow, he could not make out the light. "Long Island is low, and he had to see it to make his entry," Cooper said. "He did not want to enter the channel blind, so it's possible he dropped anchor and tried to ride the storm out.

The ship swung around to face the storm, her stern pointed to the beach. She was last seen at dark (about 4:30 p.m.) on the 16th off Ontonagon, and probably had spent less than a day coming back, so he had probably arrived at the location the next morning or before noon (November 17)."

"You can imagine the conditions on board her by that time," Cooper said. "Her canvas was frozen, seas boarded her regularly with waves rolling down the decks, and everything was ice coated. Her pumps and equipment were probably frozen — it was a really bad predicament. From what we can tell, though, they decided to drop anchor and ride it out."

He said that when divers in the 1970s entered the *Lucerne's* cabin they looked inside the cabin's pot bellied stoves, where they found the charred remnants of cabin furniture and portions of the cabin's sides. He theorized, "The crew must have used this when their coal supply had been burned up."

Cooper said that from evidence gathered later it appeared that Captain Lloyd had the centerboard down, probably to stabilize the vessel, before anchoring. But as they came about, attempting to set their hooks off Long Island, something went wrong. The anchor, or anchors, dragged or there was a critical delay in dropping them.

Captain Lloyd got closer to the shore than he wanted to.

From the charred remains in the stoves, the underwater archeologist believed that they rode about two days, the 17th and the 18th. During this time, the *Lucerne* was taking a fearful beating near shore, open and exposed to the full fury of the northeaster. Then, possibly her anchors dragged, or the capstan slipped, and the helpless *Lucerne* inched closer to the shore until her centerboard struck bottom. This opened her up and she began to sink.

Hurriedly, the crew took to the rigging, with one man up the main mast; two up the mizzen. The way two were dressed, with one man with five overcoats on but with bare feet and another with boots but without warm clothing, suggests to Cooper that they weren't ready for being out on deck. "They must have come running up on deck and dashed into the rigging. It must have happened very quickly."

He theorized that because there were no bodies found on the beach, most of the crew did not get out of the boat alive. "The forecastle probably was coated with ice, with the men trapped inside, not able to make it out before the boat sank," he said.

During an underwater exploration of the wreck, the archaeologists came across a peculiar sight: an iron bar jammed in the windlass. The windlass is a winch-like device used to control the heavy weight of the anchor, either to set it or to drag it up from the bottom. "We did not know whether they had a problem dropping the anchor or trying to keep the windlass locked." If the windlass, for example, were coated with ice, it would not let out the anchor; or, also, if it were ice-coated, it may have let the anchor rode slip — and the *Lucerne* would move closer into shore.

The crew was probably trying to drop the anchor. "Someone had probably tried to insert a crow bar to free it before the *Lucerne* was driven ashore — a desperate act," Cooper said.

The underwater evidence showed the centerboard was found pretty much knifed into the bottom at about a 30 degree angle. Cooper said, "That tells me they were moving backward, dragging anchor, and she struck bottom and broke her back." Additionally, the underwater archaeologists found a break in the keelson fore and aft of the centerboard. That quickly sank her, taking her captain and all her crew to their deaths.

In a cryptic note, the 1886 *Marine Record* analyzed final actions which might have saved the giant schooner. Had she been run ashore, the *Record* said, she might have been saved. "...but when she let her anchors go in the storm, close inshore, so that her stern wheeled around to the shore, her case was hopeless. Death to the crew was inevitable, except for a miracle, and the miracle did not come. It is probable that, in the blinding snow storm, Captain Lloyd did not know that he was so close to land or he would have taken the chance of driving her right on shore instead of letting her drag anchors in such a hurricane."

I sat back against the cockpit, feeling the wind on my back. The morning was brightening around me, making last night's adventures seem remote.

There were some parallels to think about. Like the *Lucerne*, we had been caught in a storm on a nasty coastline and had searched for an entryway, but did not immediately find it. We had the advantage of having GPS to guide us in close to our entryway, however, so we knew approximately where we were, even though we could not see through the billowing fog. We were running under twin diesels and had lots of maneuverability, where the *Lucerne* had practically none.

It came home to me once more that last night we had tiptoed along a narrow line with potential disaster looming at us.

We made it off the lake to safety.

The *Lucerne* wasn't as lucky.

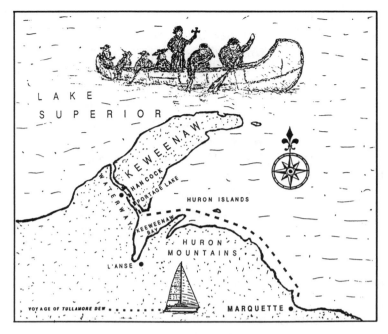

CHAPTER THIRTEEN

ON THE TRACK
OF THE
BLACK ROBES

THE TWIN DIESELS HUMMED happily at 2,800 r.p.m., enough to give us a speed of 6.8 knots as we left the marina at Hancock. We were on our way under sunny skies amid technicolor scenery, up the historic and beautiful water road of the Keweenaw waterway.

Today we'd travel to historic Portage Lake, exit the waterway into Keweenaw Bay and enter once again the open waters of the big lake. Then we'd sail past the Huron Islands along the rugged Michigan coast and, if all went well, end up in Marquette by late afternoon.

I leaned back in the cockpit of the big catamaran as my thoughts turned inward. There was a lot of history to be seen on this waterway, especially as we entered Portage Lake, part of an old route used by Native Americans and voyageurs during the fur-trading era. We'd also be following the route of the famous "black robes" of Lake Superior, the French Missionaries Father Rene Menard, and Father Frederic Baraga.

I had been looking forward to seeing historic Portage Lake on the Keweenaw ever since I read about it in *Kitchi-Gami, Life Among the Lake Superior Ojibway*. The book was written by Johann Georg Kohl, a German writer who in 1855 paddled through these very waters in a birch bark canoe.

Kohl had come from the Apostle Islands, but had to land further north on the peninsula than we did since the western entry to the waterway had not yet been constructed. He then paddled and portaged his way down to Portage Lake. This was the route used from early times to "avoid the tedious and dangerous navigation" around the tip of the peninsula to the north. It was from this waterway that the peninsula received its Native American name, Keewaynan, meaning "the way made straight by means of a portage."

Writer Kohl and everyone else in those days travelled by birch bark canoe, which had been romanticized by Henry W. Longfellow in his famous *Song of Hiawatha*. The poet rhapsodized over the canoe that floated upon the water "like a yellow autumn leaf, like a yellow water-lily."

But Kohl found the reality of the canoe "extremely unpoetical...when a trio of human bodies are stretched out on the wooden ribs of such a wretched fragile 'water lily,' made of thin birch bark, without the slightest comfort, no bench or support, nor even a bundle of hay or straw."

I could almost picture him now, paddling grumpily down these very waters, in his pack bag an Ojibway lexicon collected by a black-robed priest known as the Snowshoe Priest, who had also traveled through this area. In many ways, I was not only following writer Kohl on his journey but also was on the track of this "black robe" — as well as that of the priest who preceded *him*.

Our journey was achieved with considerably more comfort than the priests or the voyageurs had enjoyed, I noted as I relaxed on the open deck, a soft-drink bottle in my hand. Joe was at the helm, Thom was below at the bridge deck navigation station.

The fourth member of our crew, Bruce, padded his way along the deck beyond the cabin and then disappeared. I decided to follow. On the cat's large foredeck was a wide area, complete with mat and headboard — its pop-up sundeck recliner. Here Bruce was lazily sprawled out full length, his head propped up.

I plopped myself down, and after adjusting my cap low over my eyes, peered about as we glided along the waterway. I decided the sundeck was a little bit of heaven.

"Sometimes I sleep out here nights," Bruce said. "Under the stars, it can be just beautiful."

I settled in. The day was exceptionally beautiful, warm, almost tropical. Since I had nothing else to do right now, there was time for me to take in the sights and even have a little doze in the sun. The scenery glided by until around 11 a.m., when we exited the breakwater into Keweenaw Bay and the open waters of Lake Superior. I looked forward to getting under sail; wind was forecast out of the south to southwest, which would be fine reaching for the cat.

My thoughts turned back to Kohl, who had a different reaction when his birch-bark canoe party entered the bay, worrying whether they would find a "vent de terre" or a "vent du large." Kohl wrote:

"We desired the former, for as these small voitures (canoes) always glide along near the shore, like timid ducks, the wind blowing off shore (vent de terre) is preferable for them. As it has to cross the steep shore cliffs and the forest, it strikes the lake some distance off, and leaves along the coast a perfectly smooth patch of water, over which the canoe glides rapidly. The 'vent du large,' on the other hand, sends up high waves, produces a violent surf, and renders a canoe voyage often impossible."

We didn't find either, for the wind had perversely switched to the east. That meant the wind was almost on our nose — we were heading into it at an angle. Joe made his decision: up sails, anyway.

We hoisted the big mainsail, then unrolled the genoa. With a pop, it caught the wind and we cranked it down hard to set it with the winch.

We were now motorsailing, the diesels idling along while the sails drew and gave us a slight boost. We had created our own "vent," making an easy crossing of Keweenaw Bay, heading around Point Abbeye, a small point of land to the south and east.

This bay, the entry to the waterway from the east, has its own rugged history. Here explorers Pierre Esprit Radisson and Medard Chouart, Sieur des Groseilliers, paddled their birch bark canoes in 1659. They had come from Sault St. Marie — our destination — heading deeper into the wilderness of the Keweenaw Peninsula and then on to the Minnesota north shore, where a river still bears the name of de Groseilliers, Anglicized almost beyond reason to the "Gooseberry River."

Radisson's account of his adventures became a best-selling book in its day and Europeans must have been agog at this glimpse of the new world. Superior's shores were "most delightful and wounderous," with part of its south shore rocks like "a great Portall, by reason of the beating of the waves. The lower part of that oppening is as bigg as a tower." Elated with all that he saw, he had summed up grandly: "We weare Cesars being nobody to contradict us."

Radisson was not the first European to paddle through this area; years before had come Etienne Brule, one of Samuel de Champlain's men sent to explore the new country. From the Hurons, he had heard that there was a "sea of which they have not seen the end, nor heard that anyone has." Champlain had specimens of copper taken "from a bank of a river near a great lake."

Sent to investigate, Brule and his canoe party are believed to have reached in about 1623 as far westward as the Minnesota north shore. The Frenchman reported visiting a place on Superior where the Native Americans were mining copper, and brought back an ingot of copper from a region "eighty or one hundred leagues from the Huron Country." (A league is about three miles.) Brule gave the length of the great lake he was on as "four hundred leagues."

After his great canoe trip the whole length of Superior and back, Brule never returned to live in New France. As the story goes, his Lake Superior experience so changed Brule that he turned his back on European society and went to live with the Hurons, where he was killed in a knife fight over a woman. They ate his heart, which was considered to be a great honor.

I mused on what a wild adventure it must have been to be on the open waters of the big lake in a fragile, tippy, and often leaky birch-bark canoe. I remembered that one of the earliest descriptions of canoes on Lake Superior came from a Jesuit writer, who left us with this graphic account:

"It was a sight to arouse pity to see poor Frenchmen in a Canoe, amid rain and snow, borne hither and thither by whirlwinds in these great Lakes, which often show waves as high as those of the Sea. The men frequently found their hands and feet frozen upon their return, while occasionally they were overtaken by so thick a fall of powdery snow, driven against them by a violent wind, that the one steering the Canoe could not see his companion in the bow. How then gain the port? Verily as often as they reached the land, their doing so seemed a little miracle."

The earliest "black robe" to come into this area, Father Rene Menard, also had his troubles in canoes as he braved the Superior wilderness. Aging and in ill health, the French missionary had begun his journey in 1660 from New France, in Canada, in a fleet of about 60 canoes paddled by Ottawas. His task was to gain converts among the Hurons who lived along the shores of Lake Superior. Down the St. Lawrence River they came, following the traditional canoe route past Montreal, entering the Ottawa River headed westward, then paddling and portaging rivers and streams to Georgian Bay, and from there, westward across the open waters of Superior.

The canoe party forced the elderly priest to both paddle and carry packs. At one of the many portages, Father Menard slipped, injuring his foot and an arm. For the rest of the trip, he went barefoot because his foot had become infected and swollen. Following the south shore of Superior, the canoe band hugged the land so they could pull their canoes off in case of sudden storms. When the old priest's canoe was destroyed by a falling tree, the rest of the party paddled away, leaving the old priest and his party stranded on shore without food. Father Menard and his group survived by making stews from old bones and dried blood they found around an old campsite. Finally, another band of voyageurs paddled by and gave them a ride.

They voyaged past the Huron Mountains and into Keweenaw Bay, arriving on Saint Theresa's Day, October 15, 1660. Father Menard named the area after the saint, L'Anse de Sainte Therese, later shortened to L'Anse, meaning "cove."

He had spent 48 days on his journey, but the weary and injured priest was not yet at rest. The Ottawas ordered him away from camp; he had to spend the winter in a hut made of fir branches. He managed to baptize 50 inhabitants, but nine months later, he decided to follow the ancient Lac View Desert Indian Trail to another village. On the way, his Huron guides deserted him; the elderly priest was never heard from again. Somewhere, on the south shore of Superior, lies the unmarked final resting place of one of the earliest black robes on Superior.

We headed further into Keweenaw Bay. To the north of us lay Traverse Island, and, further to the East, the Huron Islands that Father Menard canoed past. It may have been one of these islands that gave rise to the legend of the "disappearing islands" of Lake Superior. Author Kohl must have seen these, or other islands, as he wrote:

"There lay a tall, bluish island, with which the mirage played in an infinity of ways during our voyage. At times the island rose in the air to a spectral height, then sank again and faded away, while at another moment we saw these islands hovering over one another in the air. That the watchful Indians not only observe this optical delusion, but also form a correct idea of its cause, is proved by the name they give to the mirage. They call it 'ombanitewin,' a word meaning so much as this, 'something that swells and rises in the air.'"

I was reminded of the phenomenon one day when I was driving along Minnesota's north shore, looking out over Superior's open waters. The distance faded into a light blue haze. The next day, to my amazement, there lay Isle Royale, the largest island on Lake Superior, about 45 miles in length and about 20 miles from Minnesota's shore. It had seemed to jump out of nowhere and lay boldly like a miniature continent off in the distance. So there was some credence to the legend of the disappearing islands of Lake Superior.

But it was not only the optical tricks of Superior that caused problems for the early explorers. I had to smile as I recalled that to the north and west of us lay legendary Isle Phelipeaux — sort of. Decades of explorers had searched in vain for this island, which had appeared first on a map drawn by a Parisian mapmaker and had been seen on a number of charts of the Revolutionary period. It was supposed to be situated off the Keweenaw Peninsula to the north, occupying a position in the lake not far from Isle Royale. The mysterious island would have been hard to miss, too: on the map, Isle Phelipeaux was nearly as large as Isle Royale.

Why hadn't anyone been able to find it? Years later, it was learned that the French map maker courted the favor of a patron by the name of Phelipeaux. Lake Superior was such a wilderness, and so far from civilization, the map maker reasoned, that if he were to draw in an extra island to honor his patron, who was to know? The map caused confusion for many years until it was finally discovered that this island was but a figment of a conniving map maker's imagination.

As our journey continued, my thoughts of the early black robes turned to yet another famous priest on Superior. To the south of us on Keweenaw Bay, in a beautifully wooded area on the red rock bluffs one mile west of L'Anse, Michigan, stands a huge statue of a priest, his face turned to look over the very body of water we were traversing. The golden 35-foot tall figure is supported on circular wooden beams rising from concrete tepees, each about 10 feet tall. In one huge hand, the statue holds a cross, and in the other, snowshoes. This is the Shrine of the Snowshoe Priest of Lake Superior, erected to honor Father Frederic Baraga's historic missionary work.

Years ago, on my first solo voyage on this lake, I had heard of Father Baraga's work on Madeline Island, where he had worked among the Ojibway of Superior and established the first permanent Catholic mission in 1835. Baraga had been an amazing man. Born in Austria, of nobility, he had heard the call of the church and was ordained after he had received his law degree at the University of Vienna. Fascinated by Native Americans, he had specifically requested an assignment on Lake Superior, where he wrote what became best-selling books in Europe about Superior and Native American culture. L'Anse became the center of his missionary work; in all he spent about

30 years on Superior, many of them traveling about the lake by snowshoe, dog team, and, of course, canoe. He traveled boldly and widely.

One day, driving my car on the North Shore, I had followed a narrow road toward the lake, off Hwy. 61 near Schroeder, Minnesota, down a steep gorge beside a swiftly moving stream. At a rocky outcropping on Superior, a granite cross boldly stood vigil. The site was known as Baraga's Cross, and the stream, the Cross River. The basic facts were that Father Baraga had come ashore after a stormy crossing and the Ojibway had erected a bark cross to mark his successful landing. I was curious about the what lay behind this sketchy information.

It was through Kohl's book that I began to understand more about Baraga's Cross, for the writer's canoe party had paddled over the same waters we were now traveling. At what was then a primitive mission at L'Anse, Kohl talked to an old voyageur, and from his interview, he wove the story of Baraga's Cross:

During the time when Father Baraga was in his mission on Madeline Island, he heard that his immediate presence was needed at a mission on the northern side of the lake along what is now the Minnesota north shore. The good Father hurriedly strode to the hut of a voyageur by the name of Dubois. He was dressed, as always, in his black robe with a gold cross on his chest, breviary in his hand and three-cornered hat on his head, and he was in a hurry. What Father Baraga wanted was no less than a birch-bark canoe voyage straight across Superior.

The voyageur was greatly concerned. The weather did not look promising and no one had attempted a crossing straight from the Apostles to the North Shore, a distance of about 70 miles of open water.

Normally, voyageurs made their passage to the North Shore along the coast in about eight days. Native Americans and voyageurs rarely made traverses across the lake greater than 15 miles from cape to cape, so that they could pull their boats ashore when bad weather threatened. Dubois knew that a passage of 25 or 30 miles was called a "grande traverse" and one of 70 miles would be called an impossibility.

But the priest prevailed. Soon he and the voyageur were in a birch bark canoe, paddling northward out of the Apostles.

Kohl's book records a voyageur, Dubois' cousin, retelling the story:

"It began to grow stormy, and the water rose in high waves. My cousin remarked that he had prophesied this, but his pious, earnest passenger read on in his breviary quietly, and only now and then addressed a kind word of encouragement to my cousin. They toiled all night through the storm and waves, and, as the wind was fortunately with them, they moved along very rapidly, although their little bark danced like a feather on the waters. The next morning, they sighted the opposite shore. But how? Long rows of dark rocks on either side, and at their base, a white stripe, the dashing surf of the terribly excited waves. There was no opening in them, no heaven, no salvation."

"'We are lost, your reverence,' my cousin said, 'for it is impossible for me to keep the canoe balanced in those double and triple breakers.'"

"'Paddle on, dear Dubois — straight on. We must get through, and a way will offer itself.'"

"My cousin shrugged his shoulders, made his last prayers, and paddled straight on, he hardly knew how. Already they heard the surf dashing near them; they could no longer understand what they said to each other, owing to the deafening noise, and my cousin slipped his couverte from his shoulders, so as to be ready for a swim, when, all at once, a dark spot opened out in the white edge of the surf, which soon widened. At the same time the violent heaving of the canoe relaxed, it glided on more tranquilly, and entered in perfect safety the broad mouth of a stream, which they had not seen in the distance, owing to the rocks that concealed it."

The priest was elated. "'Did I not say, Dubois, that I was called across, that I must go, and that thou wouldst be saved with me?"

After they had drawn their canoe ashore, the voyageur fell down on the rocks and kissed the ground. Together they went into the forest, cut down several trees, and erected a cross on the spot where they landed.

Later, a permanent cross, one that could be seen a long distance from the lake, was erected and the area came to be known as the Cross of Baraga's Traverse. Now it is simply "Baraga's Cross."

Soon we were out of Keweenaw Bay and past the Huron Islands. On our right rose the Huron Mountains, in all their rugged beauty. I suspected that these scenic, wild areas had changed little since the days of Father Baraga and Father Menard.

By 8:15 p.m., and with dark shadows settling over the hills, we were safe inside the breakwaters of Presque Isle Harbor, just north of Marquette, Michigan. Minutes later, we were tied up in the beautiful marina's clear but shallow waters. At a nearby taconite dock, a thousand-foot-long ore boat was being filled. Our voyage was completed for the day.

It had been a pleasant day's run on the lake, and for me, a rumination through some of its history, including that of two of the remarkable black robes of Superior. One died in the wilderness and lies in an unknown grave. But in Marquette, I knew, were the final remains of the Snowshoe Priest of Lake Superior. He died there in 1868 at the age of 71 and was buried in the crypt of St. Peter's Cathedral, located on Marquette's 4th and Baraga Streets.

CHAPTER FOURTEEN

VISIT TO A
BOATBUILDER

EARLY THE NEXT MORNING, we drove out of the harbor up winding roads and past heavy woods to meet Joe Bingham, a master builder of cruising sailboats. In an era in which small boatbuilders are increasingly being squeezed out, and more and more sailboat building is done by cost-efficient large corporations, Bingham is a rarity: a small boatbuilder producing quality sailboats—a veritable David among boating's Goliaths.

Suddenly, we were upon it: a large metal shed, not unlike an aircraft hanger, set in the dark pines, with a collection of other buildings to the side and beyond it. This was the home of Bingham Boat Works, Ltd., Marquette, Michigan.

The Bingham Boat Works goes back three generations to a grandfather who had a boatyard in Long Island, New York, but had to move away from the east coast and salt air for his health. He picked Michigan's Upper Peninsula because it had water and clean, fresh air. He originally worked in lumber camps and then returned to boat building after he regained his health. The present boatyard began building and repairing boats in 1930, and they were still building wooden boats when Joe Bingham began working in the family business. "I was born here," he said. "I'm 53, and you could say all my years I have been in the boat business."

I enjoyed meeting Bingham, a middle-sized man with large boatbuilder's hands, and I immediately got a taste of his quick wit: "I only work half days," Bingham joked. I must have looked surprised, for he quickly added: "Eight to eight, always 12 hours—that's only half a day."

"It's only a part-time job."

Today, the Bingham Boat Works is still a family business. Joe's wife does paperwork for the boatworks part time; a son works full time, and a daughter does upholstery. Another son and daughter-in-law also work part time. Joe and his wife have 11 children.

Under Joe's guidance, we began our tour of the plant. "You have to have a sense of humor and a thick skin to be in the boat business," he explained. "Not all boat owners are pleasant people. We deal with them all. They are like they are. Most of our business is repeat customers and they bring us more customers. Word of mouth is precious. We have to work hard and they know they get a good job here."

In one large shed, we saw two hulls under construction, with a third in the yard. I clambered up a ladder to get into a recently completed hull. It stood upright on its keel, with its interior open and ready for finishing off. I was impressed with its no-nonsense, sea-kindly look. There was a sweet sweep to the sheer, which ended in a short bowsprit, where the outer jib would be set to provide extra horsepower. The beam was 8 foot, six inches, and the draft was a minimal 3 feet, 11 inches. This was a design for a cruiser, not a racer.

I noted that in this era of boat-building superlatives, Joe referred to his craft not as a 28 or 30-footer, but simply as a 27.8. "That's the actual length on deck," he said, "leaving off the length of the bowsprit."

He said that the boat was designed to fit in a 30-foot slip, and that was important because after 30 feet in many marinas, you have to rent or buy slips for 40-footers, and "that gets a lot more expensive."

Joe considers the 27.8 to be the "maxi trailerable boat," just pushing 7,400 pounds. If it weights more than 8,000 pounds, you need a two-ton truck to pull it around," he pointed out. It is a semi-custom boat, meaning that the boatyard customizes parts of the vessel, such as the interior, for buyers.

The naval architect for the trailerable 27.8, I learned, was designer Fred Bingham (no relation to Joe), who designed some of the noted Pacific Seacraft yard's heavy-weather fleet. That was an impressive pedigree; Pacific Seacraft is recognized as one of the best production builders in the world.

"We don't compete against the big boat-building corporations," Joe explained. "Our boating clientele is different. We deal with a person that wants a particular kind of boat. A lot of what has kept our business here is that we are very flexible. For another thing, we have to enjoy less profit. We know that from the start. Everything we buy, such as an engine, is one by one, whereas Hunter may buy a truckfull. Our savings result from labor, not materials, because if you skimp on materials then you don't have the right boat."

Bingham has sailed his own boats extensively and they reflect his interests and experience on Lake Superior, a good testing ground for craft. He settled on the Fred Bingham design because of its seaworthiness (it has offshore capabilities, Bingham advertises) and its nearly full keel design. "It's a three-quarters full keel," Bingham explained, "with cutaway up front." He chose this design rather than a fin keel, for example, because he felt that for cruising "a full keel is a lot more sea kindly than a fin keel, has a better motion, and tracks better. And for trailering, it's much easier to put on and off to launch and to haul it since the full keel sits on the trailer ramp."

In terms of boat speed, Bingham says his full-keel boat, despite greater wetted surface, is surprisingly fast, and putting a Bingham 27.8 against other boats convinced him that "you're talking a difference of perhaps 10ths of a knot."

"If I had a choice in a Superior storm, I would go full keel myself," Bingham said. "It is more sea kindly and much stronger. Think about it: a fin keel is held on by just a few bolts and how long can you rack that back and forth? The full keel is part of the boat. At least the keel is going to come back home with you.

"I think the fin keel was pushed on the public, not by choice, but by production demands because it's a lot easier to manufacture. Think of it: you build a basically flat boat, jack it up, and then stick on the keel. I worked with Hunter a few years, and looked at standard fin-keel production techniques. With the scoop transom, you could walk right in; it is very easy to fit out. It is designed as a production boat."

Production at Bingham Boat Works is one at a time and limited to demand. "If we could just build one boat, and do nothing else, it would take about three months. Most of the building time is focused on the boat's inside. We can make the hull and deck in six weeks. The finishing off is the time-consuming part."

Nearly everything that is possible to be done is done at Bingham's works. "We made our own mold and we do our own laying up of the hull," Bingham said.

The hull thickness of the 27.8 cruiser is surprising: at the sheer, it is 3/8-inch thick. At the waterline, it grows to 5/8 inch, and by the time the hull flares into the keel, it measures a whopping 3/4-thick. At the very bottom, it's one inch—practically a bullet-proof boat.

Into the keel cavity, Bingham fits a 2,665-pound custom-cast lead keel, set in epoxy putty so there's no place for water. Over the lead keel go many layers of fiberglass. "That's with the idea that if you turn turtle you might want all that lead to stay where it belongs," Bingham observed.

The 27.8 is fitted out with a Westerbeke 18-horsepower diesel, which will give a respectable top speed of 7 1/2 to 8 knots. The power plant can also be a Yanmar 18 horsepower, since the engine mounts will fit either. The boat's cutter rig spreads 412 square feet of sail, a lot for a 28-footer. But Bingham points out there are three sails to meet a variety of sailing conditions. With two headsails to work with, a sailor can easily set or douse the outer jib on a roller furler. The working jib is club-footed, with reef points.

"We've had a number of people ask why the cutter rig, and I

guess it's because we prefer it. We've sailed a cutter, and when Superior kicks up its heels, you can easily reef down. There are two reef points in the main. With reef points in the working jib, Joe said, "You can put up something in nearly any kind of weather to balance off the boat."

The boat comes with a tiller, but wheel steering is available. Bingham says he prefers the tiller. "It's simple and strong. Very quick acting. Wheel steering is fine if you drive a car; but a tiller is boat to me."

Bingham says he usually sells one or two boats a year, mostly to sailors in the Superior and Great Lakes Area, though one boat is now in the Caribbean. "A physician in Michigan bought one of our 27.8 boats, sailed it for a year in Lake Michigan, then we put it on a trailer and trucked it down to Florida. His goal was to spend a couple years in the Caribbean and he's been down there ever since." The only modification the boatworks made on the boat was to add an extension to put the working jib up higher on deck, for more visibility.

As we walked around the boatyard in the bright July sunshine, talking to this fine Superior boat builder, I mentioned our stormy night arrival at the Keweenaw entryway. He nodded his head knowingly, then told me about a boat that wasn't as lucky as we had been.

"I fixed a 28-foot cat after it hit the breakwater coming in during adverse conditions," Joe said. "The skipper told me that the pier-head lights were confusing. He turned in the breakwater, but one of his hulls hit. The collision collapsed the bow on the port hull, smashing the stem back about eight inches. Fortunately he had a water-tight compartment up front. He limped in here and we fixed it."

"I can't remember his name," Bingham said, turning toward me apologetically. "A lot of customers kid me. I can't remember their names, but I always remember the names of boats." He permitted himself a small smile. "I don't fix customers, I fix boats."

As we headed back to *Tullamore Dew*, I saw a 1,000-foot-long boat near the harbor. Out of mutual curiosity, we stopped the car and walked to the water's edge. "She's taking on ore," Joe said.

I was reminded that the area has a special niche in history: this is Iron Country. To the west, in the Keweenaw where we had just sailed, it had been copper that had burst upon the attention of the world. Later, the giant Mesabi range in Minnesota had dominated world iron production.

But it was here, shortly after the copper strike, that Superior's first iron ore was discovered—and by accident.

In 1845, a government surveyor in the heavy woods and cliffs to the southwest of Marquette found his compass needle would not hold a straight course. It kept veering off sharply, and he soon found the cause: magnetism caused by an iron ore outcropping. He hefted a few chunks to look them over, but they were so heavy that he decided not to add any to his already bulging pack. He tossed them away. Who wanted to carry those chunks through the woods?

Iron in those days was no big deal — not so much a discovery as a nuisance. Tales of compass needles swinging wide because of piles of magnetic iron rocks were only really good for some amusing tales around the campfire.

But the next year, a more imaginative man, Philo Everett, of Jackson, Michigan, heard the tale. He was searching for copper, but the story of the magnetic rocks intrigued him. Local Native Americans led him to outcroppings in an area to the southwest of Marquette.

In 1845, Everett's discovery at Negaunee became the first iron mine on Superior. West of it arose the Cleveland Mine at Ishpeming, the Native American term for "high place," since this was the highest ground between Lake Michigan and Lake Superior. These were the beginnings of iron mining on the Marquette Range—in the ancient mountains of the Laurentian range, the oldest rock in the world.

The first iron ore was hauled by horse team to the port of Marquette over rough wooded roads, primarily in the winter when the roads were frozen over. In those days, there were fewer than 150 people living in the iron country. The port of Marquette's first dock was simply trees piled into the water and held down by boulders.

In 1854, only a thousand tons of ore were taken out of Marquette, and that was a winter's worth of work. It took three steamers, the *Sam Ward*, the *Napoleon*, and the *Peninsula* to transport it. The iron ore was so heavy that it was not dumped into the ship's holds, but shoveled by hand to the decks, where it would be easier to unload. It was destined for the coal-rich city of Cleveland, 800 miles from Marquette, and other iron furnaces and mills in the lower Great Lakes.

I mused over the thousand tons that took three ships to hold. Today the thousand footer we were looking at would contain between 60,000 to 70,000 tons of ore—an amount it would have taken nearly 200 boats to carry in the 1850s. One could imagine the wheelbarrows, shovels and the red-dust-covered men laboring at the dock to load up one boat, a process that took many days. The thousand footer would load her huge hull in only about 10 hours. At her destination, she would unload the ore with her elevators in about the same amount of time, sometimes quicker.

Today's long boat carried taconite pellets—concentrated iron ore. The rich iron ore from Iron Bay had run out long ago. How times changed, from when iron ore was the largest single item of commerce in the world.

We headed back to our catamaran in silence. In a short time, we'd hoist sails to resume our journey across the vast lake, so rich in history—and holding so many surprises.

CHAPTER FIFTEEN

THE STORM

JOE SWITCHED OFF the VHF weather channel and emerged into the cockpit, smiling. "Looks we can sail today," he announced.

At last! The forecast told of winds out of the southwest, steady 13 to 15 knots, with unlimited visibility. We'd be on a beam reach, a great point of sail for the catamaran. The seas of one to two feet would be no problem at all for *Tullamore Dew*.

I calculated that we would arrive at our next port, Grand Marais, Michigan, at about 6 p.m. with plenty of light — unlike the fog and the blackness we encountered at the entry to the Keweenaw Waterway. Grand Marais was a small-craft harbor and an important harbor of refuge. In fact, it was the only harbor along the 65-mile stretch of shore.

I read aloud from my *Boat Log & Record*, as I was wont to do while I began to fill out my day's sailing log. Each log page had a bit of nautical poetry, doggerel, or salty wisdom, and today's message was: "Boats are safe in harbor, but that's not what boats are for."

I thought it sounded more ominous than was really called for on such a bright, sunshiny day with a clear forecast. Still, I thought as I shrugged my shoulders, this was changeable Superior.

Joe and Bruce hoisted sails and I took over the helm. I could feel the sails billow with power as the skipper and his son adjusted them, and with nearly every twitch of a winch, the cat surged forward. This was what I had been waiting for: a high speed run in the big cat.

It was a steady, upright ride, just as if we were on rails. I realized that if I had been sailing my own boat, we'd have a considerable lean as *Persistence's* shoulder dug in and went to work — the sort of tippy way a monohull was designed to be sailed. But the wide-beamed cat stayed upright and only responded to wind gusts by jetting ahead faster.

I watched fascinated as the knotmeter piled up higher numbers: 6...7...8...8.2 knots. Hey, this is what Superior sailing is all about, I mused to myself. Wide open skies, sunshine, light seas and enough wind to make the cat fly.

By now Joe, Bruce and Thom were belowdecks. I was alone at the helm watching the compass and adjusting course as the growing breezes hit the cat. Checking the digital knotmeter, and then the GPS a few seconds later, I saw that our speed didn't fall below 6 1/2 knots, but could run up to about 8 knots quite easily in a gust. I felt elated.

Glancing to my right, I saw that the shore was bluff, with high points up to 100 feet above the lake; part of it was sheer exposed cliffs, running right to the water's edge.

Although I couldn't see them today from our course far out on the lake, I knew that somewhere over there lay the beautiful Pictured Rocks, an area where Ojibwa tradition held that gods lived. Looking at the spectacular sheer cliffs and getting a sense of the awesome feeling of nature all about, it was not difficult to understand why.

The Pictured Rocks area was spun into poetry by Longfellow in his *Song of Hiawatha*. It was here that Hiawatha lived...

> Heard the whispering of the pine-trees,
> Heard the lapping of the waters,

Sounds of music, words of wonder.

Lake Superior has produced no literature of greater renown. I remember as a schoolboy thrilling to the lines:

> By the shores of Gitche Gumeee,
> By the shining Big-Sea-Water,
> Stood the wigwam of Nokomis...
> Dark behind it rose the forest,
> Rose the black and gloomy pines-trees,
> Rose the firs with cones upon them;
> Bright before it beat the water,
> Beat the clear and sunny water,
> Beat the shining Big-Sea-Water.

In 1966, the Pictured Rocks National Lakeshore was honored by being set aside as the nation's first national lake shore.

As we sailed, I kept checking the knotmeter and saw it edging upwards. The big cat was tearing across the wave trains. It was getting windy out here, I decided as I glanced toward shore, and I saw that the waves were capped with white.

Whitecaps! We were definitely getting more than the steady, mild winds of the forecast. I watched in awe as a dark patch scoured its way across the waves — a squall coming our way.

When the gusts hit, the cat only settled down and sizzled faster across the waves.

It pleased me. Time after time, I'd play the gusts. The steering wheel had a light touch to it now, and I had to concentrate not to oversteer.

Then came a roaring in my ears. I was surprised as a big gust of wind hit and the cat really took off. We planed across the wave trains, the two hulls straddling them.

I glanced down: We were doing 9.6 knots!

It was a delightful turn of speed and I was enjoying myself. Then we came to a trough between the speeding waves that the two hulls could not quite straddle, and we dipped, first one hull, then the other. Spray flew back over the bow, splashing me.

Down below, the bounce also caught the attention of Joe and the rest of the crew. They scampered rapidly to the cockpit beside me.

"Some squall," Joe remarked, rather coolly. The hulls were pitching.

"I'd say we have gusts to about 50 knots," Thom, the ex-navy man, observed in a sort of detached fashion. "Look at the waves."

Fifty knots! A lot of wind!

Sure enough, the waves were growing larger, with troughs that let one hull dip down, while the other went skyward a few feet.

We were getting slammed about in a gut-jarring ride, but the boat's handling was impeccable. In fact, the faster we went the better the cat rode, leveling off lesser waves as she plunged ahead. But we were vibrating now, with stresses building up on the two hulls and on the bridge deck as they encountered the harsh seas.

I glanced up at the mainsail. It had a weird shape to it.

The heavy sail looked like it was being bent outward at an odd, and not happy, angle.

The boat did not heel over, as my sloop would, but stayed upright on two hulls. The sail itself was taking all of the wind's force, and was, I worried, in danger of being torn off.

"Time to reef," said Joe.

Thom took over the wheel as I went forward with Joe.

We needed to get some sail down, and the modern cat was designed with a system that would let us reef the main (take down sail) from inside the cockpit. I could see the colored line that led from the boom, through turning blocks, to the rope clutch atop the cabin's aft bulkhead. One pull, and a device like a big roller shade would revolve; the mainsail, battens and all, would slide down and turn around neatly inside the big boom. Theoretically, you could easily reef as much sail as you wanted. It just wound around the in-boom furling device.

"Let this out slowly," Joe told me, and I took hold of the halyard that would keep some tension on the main. Joe uncleated the reefing line and gave a tug.

Nothing happened. I noticed he was starting to perspire.

"Give me some slack," he ordered.

He gave it another tug, then put his 200-some pound weight into the reefing line.

The sail was stuck.

We lurched atop another tumbling wave, one hull digging in abruptly.

"Take hold of the furling line," he ordered, then moved quickly for such a big man to the cabin top, where he clung to the mast.

"Pull," he barked.

But even putting some muscle into the furling device could not budge the sail. I had a suspicion, between lurches, that we were in trouble.

Bruce brought out a screw driver as Joe attempted to force the sail into the swinging boom. With no results.

What was going on? This was an expensive in-boom furling device, and it was supposed to work in all conditions.

I thought I saw the trouble: The sail was equipped with full-length battens — fiberglass strips that run horizontal to the boom. The wind's great force had bent them wildly to one side; their curves would not fit into the straight but narrow slot designed for them.

With all this jouncing about, it would not be possible to man-handle the battens out of the huge sail.

"Give me some slack," Joe yelled, and I let out the rope clutch, presumably letting the sail fall down. It did not.

Desperately, Joe reached high to grab a big handful of sail and hauled it down quickly atop the boom. He secured the folds of flapping sail with additional line.

It didn't look too elegant, but it worked.

He jumped back into the cockpit to furl the jib. "It's a Harken," he announced. "You *know* that will work."

And it did. But even with the sails down and the diesels on, we were taking a beating. Joe and Thom consulted the charts. Though the shoreline looked fierce, there were few shoals off-shore. The underwater contours indicated gradually deepening waters, without underlying obstructions.

One of the advantages of a catamaran is that it doesn't have a large keel underneath, unlike a sailboat's fin keel. The cat, I guessed, drew only a few feet. We would do as the voyageurs and Indians in their birch-bark canoes did in a storm: head for the protection of a windward shore.

As we neared land, the whitecaps diminished and the waves thinned down. The high cliffs made the wind partly skip over the nearby water; it was the wind that was causing the wave action.

The further in we crept, the calmer the water.

We kept close watch on our depthsounder, keeping in about 25 to 30 feet. That allowed plenty of depth beneath our hulls, and in the calmer waters, we moved along easily at about six and a half knots — not what we were doing in the gusts with sails up, but we were playing it a lot safer.

Boating was a real pleasure again, and we zipped in close to the shores of the Grand Sable Sand Dunes.

Odd, I thought as I glanced toward land. We were in the north woods primeval, with some of the oldest rocks in the world, on the biggest lake in the world, and now it appeared as though we were sailing by the Sahara Desert.

Huge sand dunes towered above Superior. One bluff rose nearly 300 feet above the water. It was steep, too: nearly 35 degrees of incline. I could see the wind gusts make sandy swirls on the dune-colored bank.

"It's really smoking up there," Joe observed.

This eerie, scenic area was a vast sandbox, I thought, and impressive. A beautiful beach scene, but with few beach-goers willing to risk the wind or to dip their toes into the lake's chill waters.

By 5:30 p.m., well ahead of our estimated time of arrival, we were entering the small craft harbor of Grand Marais, Michigan, and I was looking forward to tying up and getting on land to stretch my legs.

But as we came through the breakwaters, I quickly saw that what few places there were to tie a boat along a pier or bulkhead were already taken by earlier arrivals, mostly power-boats.

We circled the public dock. No luck at all. The boats were jammed in bow to stern. We'd have to anchor out.

Slowly, we began to maneuver our way around the harbor, searching for a suitable anchorage. We wove our way around several sailboats, then headed for the western shore.

From our chart, we knew that the bottom was supposed to be sand — good holding for our anchors — and after cruising back and forth about 200 yards off, using our depthsounder, we chose a spot.

I went forward with Joe and dropped both a large Danforth and a CQR plow-type anchor, then Thom backed the cat to allow plenty of scope should a heavy blast come through.

Our concern was not that the anchors wouldn't do the job, for they were oversized and could hold a much larger boat, but that if the wind shifted, as Lake Superior winds are apt to do, we'd still have enough water under our hulls as our position changed.

An 11,000-pound catamaran would be tough to kedge off a beach.

It was done. The wind swirled back eddies in the harbor, making the big cat sway back and forth. There was also an optical illusion at this point: that the anchors were dragging. Yet I realized that there was no way the big CQR and the Danforth would do anything but burrow deeper into the sand bottom, holding us securely.

Behind us was anchored a fine-looking older sloop with a white-bearded skipper.

"Are we coming too close?" Joe hollered across the distance, which I judged to be about 100 feet at closest, as both boats swung to and fro in the gusts.

"It's your boat," the sloop's skipper responded. He shrugged and went below. He was leaving it up to us.

I studied the motion of the two boats for minutes, and it appeared at last that we were not getting any nearer. The depth sounder also confirmed we were holding steady at about 12 feet; had we slipped backward into the harbor that number would have gone up.

Joe turned on the anchor lights and we wearily trudged out of the cockpit. In the lounge, dining and navigation area, we assembled around the large settee. Through the wrap-around portlights we could see the lowering light in the west and the darkening shore. It was a glorious sunset.

Darkness came, and I spent some time on deck after supper studying the shore and the sky. I hoped the storm that was forecast didn't descend on us this evening while we were at anchor.

The cat tugged playfully at her anchors, swaying back and forth with the wind gusts. From my bunk in the main salon, I felt every motion: it was not unpleasant, like being in a hammock in a tree, rocked back and forth.

I fell asleep quickly. Hours later, I awakened, listening alertly. Something was different.

I cocked my head: there was no low moan of the mast and rigging. The boat was not cocking back and forth.

I jumped out of my sleeping bag, threw open the hatch, and stepped on deck.

The northern air was fresh and chill. The moon had risen and was a huge white orb. Off to the north, I could see the northern lights winking like a light covering of skimmed milk against the dark sky.

I turned my head, trying to feel the wind's direction on my face and ears: it still blew out of the east, but it had moderated a lot.

I padded forward in my bare feet to the bow, then reached

down to tug hard at the anchor lines. They seemed firm enough, under constant tension, and that meant the anchors were holding their own.

All was well, and I ambled back to my bunk, pulled the sleeping bag up, and went soundly back to sleep.

Tomorrow would be another day on mighty Superior.

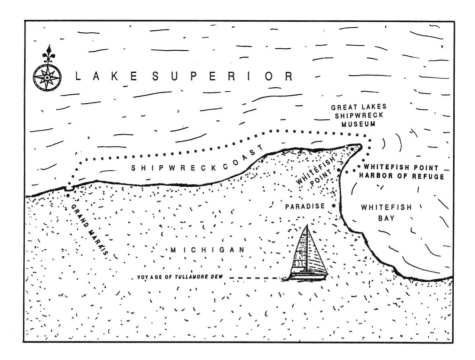

LAKE SUPERIOR

GREAT LAKES
SHIPWRECK
MUSEUM

SHIPWRECK COAST

WHITEFISH
POINT

WHITEFISH POINT
HARBOR OF REFUGE

PARADISE

WHITEFISH
BAY

GRAND MARAIS

MICHIGAN

VOYAGE OF TULLAMORE DEW

CHAPTER SIXTEEN

ALONG THE
SHIPWRECK COAST

THE NEXT MORNING, I found that the anchors had indeed held beautifully — nearly *too* beautifully — as I struggled on the bow. Joe was beside me and Thom was on the helm, following Joe's instruction to power the big cat into the wind. Trouble was, the anchors were set — hard — on the bottom.

To overcome the anchors' tenacious grip, our strategy was to take the strain off them by moving forward into the wind, though not so far that the anchor line got tangled in the props.

Joe motioned with his hand; *Tullamore Dew* surged ahead.

I tugged at one of the anchor lines, getting some slack, then Joe put the line around the forward electric capstan. He stepped on a footswitch on deck and with a powerful whir, the line tightened.

"It's down there pretty good," Joe said, almost proudly, as he motioned Thom to move the cat ahead again.

We'd use *Tullamore Dew's* heft to break loose the anchors, one by one, which were clearly set in a lot more than sand.

The big cat moved forward a bit, then hovered as Joe reeled the anchor line. Below us the anchor twisted upright, losing its grip as the cat moved over it.

The anchor broke loose, and caked with dark, heavy mud, it glided into its chock. We were free and anxious to be on our way again.

The forecast told us the winds would be switching to the west at 10 to 12 knots. As we moved past the piers into the open waters, we found that the small waves left over from yesterday's gale were lumpy and uneven.

Not enough to slow us down.

I was particularly interested in this portion of Superior and had brought a special chart on board. We were sailing along what is known as the Shipwreck Coast of Lake Superior. Here was the greatest concentration of shipwrecks on the lake.

Our nautical charts showed us that there were no major obstructions where we'd be going and that we'd have clear sailing, provided we were careful to note the shoals that extended, in some instances, a quarter to a half mile off. For the most part, though, the water below us was clear and had good depths right up to near shore.

The only problem that might arise was if we had an emergency and had to pull in somewhere for help. We were on a forlorn coastline, still nearly as wild and as undeveloped as when the first voyageurs made their way along these shores. Our destination today was a small marina on Whitefish Bay, just past Whitefish Point.

If we got in early we'd even have a chance to see an out-of-the way shipwreck museum. If we were lucky — and I emphasized the if.

So far this voyage had been anything but a milk run. This morning, after we had pulled up our anchors and briefly motored over to the Grand Marais dock for reprovisioning, we learned something that just might add more to our adventure.

Cruisers heading for the Great Lakes Cruising Club Rendezvous in Canada, at Sault Ste. Marie, warned us we might have trouble at Whitefish Point. The Whitefish Point Harbor of

Refuge was small; we discussed what we'd do if we couldn't get in: the answer was we'd just have to anchor off somewhere in the open bay.

That was, providing the weather would hold, and so far, the weather was being anything but predictable. The Whitefish Point Harbor of Refuge would be an important stopping point for us on our way to the "Soo" (Sault Ste. Marie.)

I checked our chart: there was only one other anchorage possible in the 45-mile stretch from Grand Marais to Whitefish Point.

I saw Joe turn his head about, feeling the wind on his face. "Let's give it a try," he said enthusiastically as he clambered atop the cabin to untie the sail he had so unceremoniously lashed down yesterday after it had jammed in the high winds.

Thom obligingly turned the cat into the wind.

"Haul away," Joe said, as he stood guard by the mast.

We hoisted away at the mainsail; to our surprise, it slid easily up its track to the top of the mast. As a test, we tried lowering it again. This time, though, we were under power and headed into the wind. The change in heading made the sail flog a bit, but the battens were not deformed by gale-force winds off the starboard; the sail slipped easily in and out of the roller-furling in the boom.

It was clear what had happened. In yesterday's gale-force winds, we had been trying to force the sail into the boom in the wrong manner. Conditions permitting, we should have headed into the wind, then dumped the sail.

Joe moved forward to the compartment hatch ahead of the cabin. With obvious effort, he hauled a large sail bag out, impatient to get his spinnaker up. This large head sail had more than twice the area of the mainsail, and he had put on the lines and shackles, ready to hoist, when a concerned Thom called to him: "How much wind can it hold?"

"It's rated up to about 20 knots," Joe said, impatiently.

"Look around," Thom warned. "We've got whitecaps again."

I looked around as well. The wind had silently been building back up, gusting to 25 to 30 knots.

That would tear the chute to shreds, if not overpower the boat. I saw Joe, with a disgusted look, take the spinnaker controls off, repack it, and put the big sail back in the forward compartment.

By the look on his face, I was certain we'd fly it another day.

With the wind up, we decided to learn from what we did yesterday: stay near enough to the shoreline to let the land filter out the heavy seas. We'd still have enough wind for our sails.

We decided to run a 30-foot depthline. I took over the helm and guided the cat around the underwater contours, maintaining a general course but keeping a wary eye on the depth sounder. Once the numbers started to climb upward, I headed further offshore.

Being helmsman today was simple, pleasant work and the big cat made the going easy. It was a hot July day, and I gradually took off my jacket and gloves to be in shirtsleeves.

Yet I knew today's technicolor lake was in stark contrast to what it could be.

Particularly as we cruised along Shipwreck Coast.

Shipwreck Coast acquired its name because of the large number of shipwrecks that have occurred over the years. It's also sometimes called "the graveyard of the Great Lakes."

My yellowed old chart pointed out where each wreck had occurred and where it lay underwater. This section of Superior is, without question, the worst area on the lake for shipping casualties.

The "graveyard" extended, in back of our wake, to Munising — an 80-mile stretch of inhospitable shores for the sailor, without protected anchorages or harbors of refuge in case of storms. It was impressive to see on the chart how many shipwrecks lay along the coast from Grand Marais to Whitefish Point.

I recognized the names of some of the stricken vessels; it would be hard to forget the tales of the terrible ways they went down and the many lives that were lost. There was, for example, the *Myron*, in which 16 perished when she sank 3 1/2 miles this side of Whitefish Point; and the *Superior City*, in which 29 crew members died off Whitefish Point. There were others, too, lost along this difficult and often stormy coast.

But so far, today's sail was splendid: the day was windy with blue skies and white clouds billowing above. I helmed the boat through brilliant blue water; not even gray, and nothing like the evil-looking black that sailors along this coast had experienced in storms.

At a distance, we saw many large boats cruising by, including several foreign vessels and some thousand-foot "super lakers." Some headed for the top of the lake; others were downbound. I saw that this was an area where they came close to land before steaming for the head of the lakes.

And there was something else we were approaching that I knew about.

"Out there," I said, pointing in a northerly direction, "about 15 miles away, lies the *Edmund Fitzgerald*."

I had followed the tragic story for years, from the time when I first heard the news of the freighter sinking on Superior, with a loss of all hands. In fact, she had sunk so quickly she did not even have time to cry out for help.

Now the *Fitzgerald* lay under 500 feet of water off our port side, with all her crew, for their bodies have never been recovered.

By 3:30 p.m., we had rounded Whitefish Point. It was still blowing 30 knots or more as we entered the breakwaters at Whitefish Point Harbor of Refuge, located about a mile southwest of the point. I looked ahead at the small harbor with only nine slips, most of which were used by local boaters and commercial fishermen — and I hoped we'd get a slip for the night.

As we got closer, I saw that there was one slip left open — about 17 feet wide between the breakwall and the last finger pier. I swallowed hard. We'd have barely enough room to squeeze the 15-foot-wide cat in — a piloting problem made especially difficult with the high crosswinds.

Throughout the voyage, Thom had been demonstrating to Joe how to use the cat's twin engines for various kinds of maneuvers, based on counteracting the screws. With one screw forward, and the other in reverse, Thom could set up combinations that would let the boat maneuver sideways and point in various directions. It was an old Navy method used to overcome the large amount of windage on the big cat.

Now he'd get his chance. Joe handed the helm to Thom, who maneuvered the big cat forward before turning into the 30-knot crosswind. Joe's concern was evident as the boat edged forward. I noticed water exiting under the hull in unusual streams.

Thom was applying an overpowering twist which allowed him to move the boat forward while counteracting the high winds. Finally, with a foot to spare on either side, we were in the slip.

Thom had steered a near-perfect line. The bow and then the stern was secured. "I knew you could do it," Bruce said.

As I helped cross-tie the cat between the outer wall and several pilings, I glanced around. This tiny harbor was a great place for a small vessel such as ours to take refuge behind fortress-like corrugated iron sheets, reinforced with stone walls. We were secure for the night.

As the afternoon shadows lengthened, Joe, Bruce and I hiked out of the marina, past the pine woods and onto a snaky little road to begin making our way to the point. The day was pleasant; birds sang in the deep woods that came down to the road. The occasional car whizzed past.

We rounded one bend, and ahead of us jutted the unmistakable shape of an old lighthouse. This was the former Coast Guard lighthouse built in 1849 — the oldest on the lake — and around it clustered several other buildings, all in white, tucked just behind the sand dunes. As we neared, I could see part of the remains of an old wooden schooner: an ancient wooden rudder that must have reached 25 feet in length.

Out front, a sign proclaimed that this was the Great Lakes Shipwreck Museum.

As I entered the nearest building, three SCUBA divers hovered over the bones of a wreck. I moved closer, fascinated at the realistic display: yes, these timbers actually were from an old wooden steamship. The "divers" wore authentic SCUBA gear, as they hung from the ceiling.

As I stood looking over the frames, ribs and some of the planks, it almost seemed as if I were a part of an actual dive in progress on an old sunken ship. I looked closer: this was once the *Independence*, the first steamship on Lake Superior, built in 1853, but which blew up on Whitefish Bay.

I moved on to other display areas, and I saw artifacts of other ships brought up from the Shipwreck Coast's bottom. The displays traced the history of the area's wrecks from the first identifiable sunken vessel in 1816 up to the mysterious sinking of the famed *Edmund Fitzgerald*. Each wreck exhibit was displayed with an illustration or photo of the ship when it was still on the surface and had a brief retelling of the circumstances of the tragedy. It was a well-planned, tasteful manner of bringing alive the area's colorful history using some of the artifacts that once lay unseen on Superior's dark bottom.

The Shipwreck Museum tells the story of the price the early mariners paid to ply the waters of this lake. Some were lost in devastating gales; some met their end in fog-shrouded collisions. There had been times of wild and mountainous seas and billowing black water. Ice. Sub-zero cold. Ships that pitched and rolled down to their gunwales. Furious winds. Spray that rattled against the wheelhouses, blinding captains. And along Shipwreck Coast lurked deadly rock formations — jagged ship-destroying nightmares — that reached out for the unwary.

The stories of the lost ships came alive in my mind as I moved from exhibit to exhibit. Here was one of the best displays of preserved underwater artifacts and history I have ever seen.

The museum is the work of the curator and founder, Thomas L. Farnquist, who began SCUBA diving in 1972 and quickly became obsessed with the sport. He was a science instructor, teaching school during the winter but spending summers following his passion: searching for and diving on underwater wrecks along the shipwreck coast. In 1978, he founded the Great Lakes Shipwreck Historical Society and began the Shipwreck Memorial Museum here alongside the abandoned lighthouse.

The early days of the museum must have been lean, I thought, in this out-of-the-way location. Visitors have to drive along the long, lonely road to the sandy tip of the peninsula jutting into Superior. By road, it's 11 miles north of Paradise, the nearest small community, and 33 miles from Highway 28.

In 1983, the society signed a long-term lease and began rebuilding and restoring the former Coast Guard buildings into the museum. It is now in the process of adding the abandoned Coast Guard lighthouse.

By Farnquist's own reckoning, he and his diving partners have located 25 "virgin" — meaning previously unlocated and untouched — wrecks.

"We saw artifacts disappearing — and we wanted to keep them at Whitefish Point or at least in Michigan," he told me, explaining that in earlier decades some SCUBA divers pillaged wrecks to bring back souvenirs of their dives. However, in 1980, a state law was passed prohibiting amateur divers from taking anything from the ships they found on the bottom. Now, only museums can remove selected items, and then only after obtaining a permit. They also have to develop a salvage plan, a conservation plan, and a public exhibition schedule.

"The vast majority of people will never visit shipwrecks," explained Farnquist, telling his vision of the role of his museum. "Some artifacts that are representative of shipboard life or identifiable from a vessel should be recovered if there is a good conservation plan and a plan for proper exhibition and care. We certainly would not want to recover everything from a wreck, only a few select artifacts that represent the human history and uniqueness of the vessel. This wouldn't take away from the vessel's integrity as a dive site for other divers."

As a former diver myself, I wondered how he found so many wrecks. He told me he begins by researching early newspaper accounts and then "putting an x on the chart" where he calculates the wrecks might be located. After that, it's a matter of systematically searching the bottom, primarily using side-scan sonar.

So that Farnquist and his divers can get to and from a potential wreck site, the Society revamped a 40-foot Coast Guard picket boat, powered by two 671 diesels, with a top speed of about 20 m.p.h. "When we acquired the boat from the Coast Guard, it was bare bones and the engines were pretty tired," he said. The society had them rebuilt completely, adding about 50 more horsepower. They repainted the steel hull and added electronics, including through-hull sonar scanners, so that

Farnquist and his divers can search an area fairly quickly.

Over the years, the ex-Coast Guard vessel has proven to be a good sea boat on Superior. "We've outrun a number of storms," Farnquist said, "but several times had to run for our lives. One year we had unusual storms come up in July out of the northwest. Around here, the storm we dread is the northwester, since that sweeps over the entire length of the lake, building up waves on this end.

"Suddenly, we had waves that were 10 to 15 feet high; we tried to run, but the following sea came too quickly, running over our fantail. We couldn't make it back around to the protection of Whitefish Point, so the only thing to do was to take the waves on the quarter, and run for Little Lake Harbor, about 12 miles west of Whitefish Point. We made it OK, though with difficulty.

"If you are on this lake long enough," he concluded, "there will come a time when you will have trouble getting off it and into a safe harbor."

I asked Farnquist how this part of Lake Superior acquired its reputation for being "The Graveyard of the Great Lakes." He told me that he estimated that of the 550 shipwrecks on Lake Superior, the Shipwreck Coast accounts for 150 to 200, "depending on what you measure."

He explained that most shipwrecks occurred around the turn of the century and involved accidents in which some boats were recovered, but that others were total losses, with calamitous loss of life, and the ships are still on the bottom. Other ships simply disappeared into the lake and were never located, though evidence of their passing, such as bits and pieces of the ships, eventually washed up on shore.

Farnquist ranked the nearby wreck of the *Myron* as one of the Shipwreck Coast's worst accidents.

It had been a bitter November in 1919, when the 186-foot-long lumber hooker *Myron* was caught in the shipmasters' nightmare, a black northwester. November is traditionally the most dangerous time for vessels on Superior's open waters; it is during these last runs of the season before shipping ends that the lake can lash out with gales of particular viciousness.

Mauled by hard waves, the 676-ton wooden hooker began to spring her planks and to leak badly. Captain Walter F. Neal made a fateful choice: there was nowhere to run, so he decided to inch his way around Whitefish point to find sanctuary in sheltered Whitefish Bay.

About a mile and a half northwest of Whitefish Point, the battered *Myron* lost power. Water crept up her bilges to extinguish her boiler's fires; her steam-driven engine slowed to a halt. The *Myron* wallowed helplessly in the battering waves.

Captain Neal gave the order for the 16-man crew to go to her two lifeboats. Four minutes later, the *Myron* sank. As the dark waters closed over her, the high piles of rough lumber on her decks wrenched free. The two lifeboats began to be punched about by the wave-tossed log jam, threatening to sink them.

Nearby, the steel ore carriers, the *Adriatic* and the *H. P. McIntosh*, drove toward the wreckage. The *Adriatic* stood off, but the *McIntosh* edged close enough to throw lines to the ice-covered survivors in the lifeboats.

In the numbing waters, the *Myron's* crewmembers could not catch and hold the icy lines. Finally, in danger herself from the near shore and the pounding timbers in the waves, the *McIntosh* reluctantly withdrew to safety.

In the meantime, a lifeboat crew from the life-saving station at Vermillion Point pursued the *Myron* in the heavy seas. After several heavy thumps, the Life Savers decided that their small wooden lifeboat could not survive the battering of the wave-tossed lumber. They withdrew.

Another drama unfolded back at the *Myron*. After the captain ordered his crew off in the ship's lifeboats, he wearily clambered into the pilothouse, then slammed the door behind him. He had decided to go down with his ship.

The waters rose in front of him as the *Myron* sank — then, suddenly, he was splashing atop the waves again. The pilothouse roof had burst off and an amazed Captain Neal pulled himself atop the floating debris.

From his perch, he saw his crewmembers entombed in ice and pounded by the churning lumber jam — but all he could do was clutch his wave-washed raft. He was blown about for 20 hours, when fate again took a hand.

In Whitefish Bay, a steamer searching for bodies saw something lying atop a bit of low-lying wreckage. The steamer's captain hoisted his binoculars, then as he ordered his ship closer, he saw that the body moved.

Soon the half-dead Captain Neal was on board, suffering from exposure and hypothermia. He was safe, but the lifeboats were nowhere to be found. Eventually, the *Myron's* 16 crewmembers' frozen bodies, still clad in their ice-covered life jackets, were recovered from the beach.

The worst collision in Lake Superior's history, Farnquist told me, happened a year later about 4 1/2 miles from Whitefish Point. There had been no howling winds or pounding waves; this time the accident happened in clear weather.

At twilight, August 20, 1920, the *Superior City*, filled with iron ore out of Two Harbors, Minnesota, neared the track of the fast steamer, the upbound *Willis L. King*. Lookouts on both vessels reported to their skippers; the boats exchanged signals. One sounded a port passing; the other starboard. Suddenly, Captain Edward Sawyer, realizing that the vessels were on a collision course, swung his vessel away and sounded the alarm.

But it was too late: the *Superior City* was rammed hard by the *Willis L. King*, rending a hole in her port side. The crew raced to the stern section, above the engine room, where the lifeboats were kept. Superior's chill waters slammed into the stricken vessel's red-hot boilers. The *Superior City* exploded, tearing away the stern section, hurtling the crew into the air.

Within two minutes from the time she was first hit, the *Superior City* sank beneath the waves with the loss of 29 lives. Only four were saved.

The lake still holds some mysteries that Farnquist would like to solve, including the mystery of the ghost ships of Superior: the *Inkerman* and the *Cerisoles*. Both ships were ocean-going minesweepers of the French Navy that sailed away from shore but never reached the next port.

Their inexplicable loss began November 24, 1918, when three steel minesweepers, built at Fort William, Ontario, Canada, sailed out of Thunder Bay, on the northern shores of Lake Superior. They were under the command of French Naval

Lieutenant De Vaisseaux Leclerc, who took the lead on board the *Sebastopol*. All three vessels had Lake Superior pilots on board and confidence was high. Their orders were to sail across Superior, make passage through the Great Lakes, and then cross the North Atlantic to France.

True, it was November on the Big Lake, but the tough 143-foot minesweepers were designed and built for ocean going. The vessels displaced 630 tons, had a beam of 22 1/2 feet, drew 13 1/2 feet, and each had four watertight compartments. Their top speed was around 12 knots; each minesweeper was armed with two heavy four-inch guns, one forward and one aft.

About 24 hours out of Thunder Bay, the minesweepers encountered a Superior gale. A blizzard blinded, then separated them. The *Sebastapol* headed around Keweenaw Point for protection. The storm was so severe that several of the *Sebastapol's* seams had broken: she was taking on water and the pumps were on continuously. Lieutenant Leclerc and his *Sebastopol* limped into the Soo on Nov. 26, and waited for the rest of the fleet.

But the two other minesweepers had simply disappeared.

An extensive search of Canadian and the U.S. shores found no trace of the missing vessels, their 76-man crews, nor the Canadian pilots. It was as if the steel ships had fallen into a hole in Superior; later stories had speculated that the missing minesweepers had entered a northern version of the "Bermuda Triangle," into which ships sail and never return. No wreckage has ever been positively identified as coming from the lost ships.

Today, some experts surmise that the minesweepers were brought down by heavy seas near the Keweenaw Peninsula. But Farnquist thinks that the vessels might lie anywhere between the Keweenaw and Whitefish and "we suspect closer to the Keweenaw."

He has researched as much of the vessels' voyage as he can, the same way he did the other wrecks he has found, and from his vantage point atop Whitefish Bay, he has listened to tales of fishermen and others who work on the lake. He notes that an unpainted lifeboat that might have been off one of the French vessels came ashore near Big Two-Hearted River, along Shipwreck Coast.

Another clue came when a fisherman told him about a human skeleton found on Michipicoten Island, to the northwest of Whitefish Point. It still wore a French naval officer's uniform.

It's possible that somewhere on the bottom between the rugged shipwreck coast and the island to the north may lie the ill-fated French vessels.

"We hope to look for them," Farnquist said. "Imagine finding the mine sweepers complete with their cannon down in the depths."

There is another Superior mystery that fascinates Farnquist: the disappearance of the 245-foot steamer, the *Bannockburn*, the "Flying Dutchman" of Lake Superior. In her era, she was as famous a lost ship as the sunken *Fitzgerald*, though the *Bannockburn* has never been located.

The sturdy 1,620-ton steel steamer was built in Great Britain in 1893, sailed across the Atlantic, and was regarded as a well-constructed, seaworthy vessel. On November 20, 1902, she was on a late, if routine, run out of Port Arthur, Ontario, with her hull filled with 85,000 bushels of Canadian wheat.

A terrible mid-lake Superior storm caught her. Two Canadian ships reported sighting the *Bannockburn* northeast of the Keweenaw Point, heading eastward, but that was the last time she was ever seen. The Canadian steamer simply went missing and her crew of 20 disappeared with her.

Farnquist notes that wreckage, including a life jacket bearing the ship's name, washed up on the shores near Grand Marais. That might be a clue that the *Bannockburn* lies somewhere off Shipwreck Coast.

Why did Whitefish Point become "Shipwreck Point" — the entrance to Shipwreck Coast?

Farnquist explained that Whitefish marks the turning point for all ships, either entering or leaving Whitefish Bay — where shipping lanes come dangerously close to one another. There were a lot of collisions, in fog, storms, and even smoke from forest fires.

"There also was nowhere to hide in the storms," he pointed out, "except at Whitefish Point or Grand Marais, which is difficult to get into. Remember, too, that there are 350 miles of open lake and the prevailing winds are out of the northwest, especially in November, when so many ships run into trouble."

I left the Shipwreck Museum, impressed. This was a place of history and awe.

But there was something else here that fascinated me. I walked past the old Coast Guard lighthouse —the light that failed one tragic night — and over the sand dunes to the water's edge.

A chill wind greeted me. From here, I could see far out onto Superior.

Out there, in more than 500 feet of cold water, lay the greatest shipwreck mystery of them all.

CHAPTER SEVENTEEN

THE MYSTERY
OF THE EDMUND
FITZGERALD

THE CHILL WATERS of the world's largest freshwater lake
stretched out to infinity on the horizon. I was at Whitefish
Point, on the famed Shipwreck Coast, and out there was a
grave — the resting place of the victims of Lake Superior's
most baffling and infamous maritime mystery. I could see the
approximate position at which the *Edmund Fitzgerald* sank
November 10, 1975, only 17 miles out. She was that close to
safety.

Her captain and crew were trying to make out this shore
through the storm-lashed lake. I knew from reports of their
radio dispatches that they had been anxiously scanning for this
wind-scoured tip of land, but to no avail.

Directly behind me rose the Whitefish Point lighthouse, whose beacon was to have guided the big ship to safety. But the lighthouse was black that fatal night; the terrible storm had ripped out the lighthouse's electricity.

Not that it mattered, anyway: the *Edmund Fitzgerald* and all her crew had plunged to the depths before she reached this shore. She sank so quickly there was no time to cry out for help. Now she lies beneath Superior's cold deep blue.

No one wanted to believe that she could have sunk the way she did. It seemed inconceivable that any lake storm, however powerful, could bring her down. After all, the *Fitzgerald* was a steel ship; her sheer size and modern construction made her seem indestructible. She was the finest creation of the hand and mind of humans and designed to take on anything that nature could throw at her.

She was celebrated as the queen of the fleet, rating a salute from other vessels, and she set records for speed and tonnage. She was a great ship, even regarded as a "lucky"vessel. And she became the *Titanic* of the Great Lakes.

On the 10th of November, the *Fitzgerald* was not alone on the lake. She started out in the company of several other ships that, although caught in the worst storm of the season, survived. She and another ore carrier, the *Anderson*, battled increasingly awesome waves up from the head of the lake, along the Minnesota North Shore, then down the Canadian side of the lake, to within 17 miles of safety on the eastern end, where I now stood.

Had she gone just a little further, around Whitefish Point, she would have had shelter from the storm. She would have been out of the northwester's waves; she possibly could even have run up in the shallows, near a beach.

The two skippers out on that lake who had been in contact with the *Fitzgerald* during her last hours verified in graphic terms the power of this inland sea in a storm. One told me of the lake boarding his vessel like a tidal wave. Another recalled some of the last words of the *Fitzgerald* over the ship's radio. The *Fitzgerald's* skipper had his microphone on, as if to send a message, but turned to scream to the crew, "don't let them out on deck!"

Just a few hours later, the *Fitzgerald* and all her crew were lost forever in Superior's depths. It was one of the worst disasters on the big lake; the financial loss alone was the greatest in the history of all the Great Lakes.

The sinking of the *Edmund Fitzgerald* has been exhaustively researched over the years. Millions of dollars and countless manhours have been spent on underwater probes in attempts to reconstruct the great marine tragedy. The official inquiry was a massive effort, the most comprehensive investigation ever into a Great Lakes maritime disaster.

The *Fitzgerald's* underwater wreck was surveyed and examined many times. The investigations started in the spring of 1976, when the Coast Guard plumbed the depths of Superior's dark waters with its *CURV-III* submersible to bring back videotapes and still pictures of what lay in the darkness at 530 feet. It was an extensive investigation. Enlargements of the videotape showed some details, including a large hole in the *Fitzgerald's* bow, that had not been expected.

In 1980, the French explorer Jacques Cousteau, on board his famed *Calypso*, sent down his yellow submarine, but it had barely reached the level of the *Fitzgerald's* pilot house when its electric motors failed and it had to resurface. Disappointingly, it did not report anything significant.

In 1989, the Great Lakes Shipwreck Historical Society began a series of seven dives in three days using a remote controlled unmanned submersible that shot 3-D videotape. The robot peered inside the still-intact pilothouse, sending back images of articles of clothing and telephone receivers hanging from their cords. It also revealed a hole several feet wide, on the starboard bow. Its edge was jagged, as if the metal had been torn outward, not punched inward — contributing to the mystery.

In 1994, a 22-foot research submarine, the *Clelia*, sank beneath Superior's dark waters to take explorers, including Tom Farnquist of the Great Lakes Shipwreck Historical Society, down to the *Fitzgerald*. One of the other participants in the expedition was also involved in dives on the *Titanic*; the expedition used the same type of lights that were used on the *Titanic* dive.

Like a helicopter, the sub hovered over the wreck, then

darted up to peer into the pilot house from which Captain Mc-Sorley sent his last message, "We are holding our own."

Later, from their base onboard the scientific research ship, the *Edwin Link*, marine historians and fellow marine scientists from the Harbor Branch Oceanographic Institution, in Fort Pierce, Florida, used state-of-the-art imaging technology to scrutinize some of the clearest views ever of the wreck.

In July, yet another submarine sank in Superior's ghostly darkness. Fred Shannon, a Michigan businessman and adventurer, announced a startling find: a body, probably one of the 29 crewmen who went down with the *Fitzgerald* in 1975. No bodies had been reported on previous videotaped remotes or other excursions, though it was widely believed that crewmen were entombed inside the wreck. The submarine left the body where it lay, in an area near the bow section outside of the wreckage. Shannon notified the Canadian government.

The dives, videos and in-person explorations showed the amazing condition of the *Fitzgerald* wreck, virtually unchanged after 20 years underwater. Ships that go down in salt water become corroded and rot away, but Superior's cold fresh water helped preserve the *Fitzgerald*. Video footage shows the paint still intact and the name clearly visible.

The wreck lies in two distinct pieces: the stern, upside down, and the forward section, still upright as if sailing on. In between is a junkyard.

The 276-foot long forward section is the best preserved. The violence of her final plunge to the bottom broke all but three of her pilot house windows — one portside chart room window and two stern chart room windows are still intact. She suffered tremendous damage, with torn and twisted sections, indicating a bow-first collision with the bottom at great speed.

Despite the evidence brought back by these explorations, the mystery remained. What exactly caused the sinking of the *Fitzgerald*?

At 3:20 p.m. that fateful day, Captain Cooper, who had been following the *Fitzgerald* on his radar, peered hard into the *Arthur Anderson's* radar console along with Second Mate Roy T. Anderson.

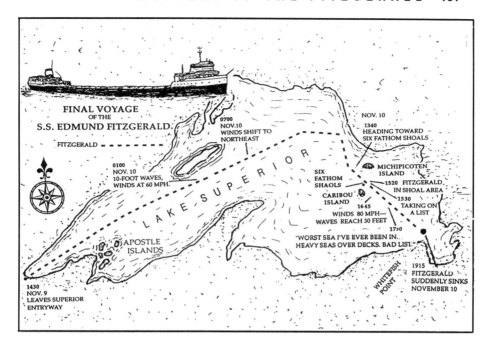

FINAL VOYAGE
OF THE
S.S. EDMUND FITZGERALD

FITZGERALD - - - - -

0100
NOV. 10
10-FOOT WAVES,
WINDS AT 60 MPH.

0700
NOV.10
WINDS SHIFT TO
NORTHEAST

NOV. 10

1340
HEADING TOWARD
SIX FATHOM SHOALS

MICHIPICOTEN
ISLAND

SIX
FATHOM
SHOALS

1520 FITZGERALD
IN SHOAL AREA

CARIBOU
ISLAND

1530
TAKING ON
A LIST

1645
WINDS 80 MPH—
WAVES REACH 30 FEET

1730
"WORST SEA I'VE EVER BEEN IN.
HEAVY SEAS OVER DECKS. BAD LIST."

LAKE SUPERIOR

APOSTLE
ISLANDS

WHITEFISH POINT

1915
FITZGERALD
SUDDENLY SINKS
NOVEMBER 10

1430
NOV. 9
LEAVES SUPERIOR
ENTRYWAY

"Look at this," Captain Cooper said, nodding to the small dot registered on the radar screen. "It's the *Fitzgerald*. He's in close to that Six Fathom spot."

Second Mate Anderson clicked the selector knob to bring the scope's range in closer. "He sure looks like he's in the shoal area."

"He's in too close," Captain Cooper said, adding quickly, "He's in closer than I'd want this ship to be."

Captain McSorley had indeed cut a tight corner over the Six Fathom Shoals. These deadly reefs, extending about five miles north of Caribou Island, lay near the route of the northern trek the big boats took when the weather turned bad on Superior. He had wanted to get in the shadow of the island to give his boat some relief from the waves which scoured his aft section with black water. The Six Fathom Shoal area was well-known to lake captains on the storm-bound northern trek — others had strayed too close and had touched bottom there — and in milder weather had been lucky enough to come away with nothing worse than slight bottom damage.

Captain McSorley was known as a "weather captain" who would push his vessel despite weather and waves. But for the last several seasons, he had been concerned about his big *Fitz*.

Built in 1958 as the largest vessel on the lake, she was now an aging ship that had been used hard. Captain McSorley knew she wasn't indestructible; he worried aloud about her "wiggling thing," as he put it. All big ore boats flex in heavy waves, but the *Fitzgerald's* bow "wiggled." One former crew member described it as "like a diving board after somebody has jumped off." Sometimes it didn't straighten out until several minutes later.

Moreover, the *Fitzgerald* groaned with her movements, even in relatively calm waters. During one winter inspection, crew members reported being down in her bilge with a shipyard foreman when he had shoved a crowbar between the keel and the hull — where they should have been welded together. Instead of a solid, continuous weld, the keel had been welded to the hull during construction with small tack or strip welds. Some of the welds, they saw, were cracked or broken. The *Fitzgerald* had what was called a "loose keel."

With her huge length, her inherent flexibility must have set in motion dynamics and stresses that were enormous. As she twisted about in rough weather, she may have loosened or fractured frames and bulkheads. Under the loose keel, she may have caused fractures or weakened her bottom's steel plates.

Repairs had been made during the winter season of 1972-73, but these merely added small steel bars to fill in the gaps between the keel and the hull before welding them together. The crew worried; they felt the hull wasn't fully repaired.

The legal limit for the load line was increased in 1973, which permitted the ship take on increased cargo, putting more stress on the weakened hull. The *Fitzgerald* rode deeper in the water; the "wiggling thing" got worse.

Sometime about a year later, the *Fitzgerald* showed up with a great crease along her starboard section, up high. How did the dent occur? The damage was too high up on the hull to have been caused by rubbing a lock wall or powering through an ice field.

It was a major dent; if the hull had rubbed on anything, it would have been along the sheer strake, a major structural member. Could the bent plates represent major losses in hull strength? Were the frames loosened from the hull — and fractured as well?

At about 3:20 p.m., there was probably no question in Captain McSorley's mind that he had "touched"somewhere in Six Fathom Shoals.

As he put distance between Caribou Island and the *Fitzgerald's* stern, at 3:35 p.m. — fifteen minutes after Captain Cooper had seen the *Fitzgerald* in the Six Fathom Shoal area — Captain McSorley radioed a message to the *Anderson*:

"*Arthur M. Anderson*, this is the *Fitzgerald*. I have sustained some topside damage; I have some fence rail down, two vents lost or damaged, and I have taken a list. I am checking down."

Captain Cooper, on board the *Anderson*: "Do you have your pumps going?"

"Yes, both of them," McSorley snapped.

Captain Cooper knew that the *Fitzgerald* had suffered severe leakage, but not from topside damage. The broken vents could let in some water, but not enough to cause the *Fitzgerald* to have a list. There was something terribly wrong down below; the *Fitzgerald's* pumps could throw out a total of 32,000 gallons per minute.

What could have happened? There were three clues: The broken fence rail, the broken vents, and the list.

Broken fence was significant: it meant that the steel cable along the spar deck had snapped; a wave coming on board could not have caused that. Vents were broken — heavy steel castings, looking in their massiveness like fire hydrants.

Both the broken steel cable and the broken vents probably meant that the hull had "hogged"— flexed, bending upward in the center. The steel cable had probably broken when impact had thrown the hull upward with terrible force — enough to tear the steel cable in half.

Waves coming aboard had nothing to do with the breaking of the vents, either. The ballast tank vents were heavy duty, cast-iron pipes, standing about a foot off the deck. These pipes led down into ballast tanks to equalize pressure when ballast was being filled or pumped out. If the ship's bottom had hit a reef, the pipes could have jammed upward, snapping off.

Lastly, the ship had list. Captain McSorley himself probably wondered how many tons of water in a 729-foot ship carrying 26,116 tons of taconite would cause a list to starboard.

Added together, fifteen minutes after she passed through Six

Fathom Shoals, the *Fitzgerald* was in deep trouble — and her captain and crew knew it.

At about 5:30 p.m., when winds were gusting to a reported 96 m.p.h., with wave heights of 30 feet, Captain McSorley made contact with Captain Cedric Woodard. Captain Woodard was the pilot on board the upbound Swedish freighter, the *Avafors*, off Whitefish Point and taking a terrific pounding. "We are taking heavy seas over our decks," the *Fitzgerald's* captain said in a strained voice. "It's the worst sea I've ever been in."

On the *Anderson*, miles behind the *Fitzgerald*, giant waves were overrunning her stern, washing down the spar deck. The boat had green water standing as high as 12 feet on the spar deck, making it seem more submarine than ore carrier.

A wave, bigger than all that had yet been encountered, slammed over the stern, burying one lifeboat atop the aft cabin. The wave rolled up the spar deck to pile up behind the pilot house in a solid wall of water.

"Just don't look back," one officer told a member of the crew. Two hundred feet behind the first came a second wave — even higher at 35 feet — that now slammed into the boat, this time putting green water onto the bridge deck. The bow buried, then recovered; they prayed the vessel would hold together.

The waves hit the *Anderson* about 6:30 p.m. Captain Cooper took stock: the *Anderson* had survived but the storm waves had damaged a life boat and bent and torn parts of her steel hull's superstructure.

Ahead, and directly in the path of the deadly waves, was the laboring *Fitzgerald*.

The last the *Anderson* saw of the vessel in front of her was at 7:10 p.m., when the *Fitzgerald's* radar image was obscured by sea return and snow squalls.

By 7:15 p.m., she was gone.

It was probably a deadly combination of problems that dealt the *Fitzgerald* its fatal blow. The unusual waves alone probably could not have sunk the *Fitzgerald*, any more than the *Anderson*. But when the waves came on board, the *Fitzgerald* already had massive problems that began when she hit something in the Six Fathom Shoal area: she had fence rail down, vents broken, and a list. She was taking on water.

Her huge pumps were on, but they could not keep up with internal flooding. The giant ship probably groaned anew with each wave. The dreaded wiggling thing was back, too, as the *Fitzgerald's* bow was repeatedly buried under tons of water, then exerted buoyant upward pressure even as tons of cargo in her hull levered the ship downward.

Captain McSorley probably knew he was in trouble, but the only thing to do was run for it — into the safety of Whitefish Bay.

He was within 17 miles of safety when the waves piled on board. The towering first wave slammed into the aft section, then rolled the length of the spar deck to pile high behind the pilot house. Captain McSorley must have looked back at the looming green water; he must have felt the shudder and the thrust as the wave crashed by.

Moments after the first, came the second, and even larger, wave. The weight of the waves on board the boat, piling up behind the pilot house, was probably enough to shove the bow down — and never let it come back up. She nose dived, probably bending forward under the terrible stresses. Inside the 729-foot hull, built without watertight bulkheads, tons of taconite shifted forward, further weighing the bow.

Still under power, the boat bored downward into the dark depths.

She submarined so quickly that her radio operator did not have time to send out a Mayday signal.

In the pilot house, McSorley and his crew must have witnessed dark waters rear skyward, then slam back through the pilot house glass, quickly crushing out all life. In the aft section, the men probably were not so lucky. Many of them had likely gathered for supper and were sitting around the galley table when there was a sudden tilt, a great lunge downward, and then a blackout as electricity was cut. There may have been pockets of air inside the steel walls to sustain life for a short while in the cold and the darkness.

Intact, the boat plunged downward, her wheel still turning, until the bow smashed into the bottom mud, digging a trench as it went in about 25 feet deep and hit bedrock. Then it jolted upward again, severely twisting the hull.

Twenty-six thousand tons of taconite exploded forward and

outward, shattering the *Fitzgerald's* cargo holds and spreading wreckage over a two-acre area. The aft section, still turning her huge propeller, twisted about, then fell deck-down into the silt, her bottom pointing heavenward.

After that fateful November 10, the search for clues to her sinking began with a desperate intensity, fanned by newspaper headlines and television coverage. All sought to answer the question of how a modern steel ship could sink — and under such mysterious conditions.

The official government findings came in *The Marine Casualty Report,* a 107-page document which summed up by saying that "the most probable cause of the sinking was the loss of buoyancy resulting from massive flooding of the cargo hold. This flooding most likely took place through ineffective hatch closures. The vessel dove into a wall of water and never recovered, with the breaking up of the ship occurring as it plunged or as the ship struck the bottom."

Early examinations were of the wreck itself. It wasn't until the following year, when the Canadian Hydrographic Service made the first official survey of the Six Fathom Shoals area since 1918, that investigators learned conclusively what it was the *Fitzgerald* might have hit. The survey's electronic data showed not one reef, but a series of reefs running throughout the area, some as little as 5 1/4 fathoms deep, and covering a wider area than previously believed to have existed. One lay about a mile farther east than any in the Six Fathom Shoal cluster that was depicted on either Canadian or U.S. navigation charts.

The newly verified shoal, the Lake Carriers Association pointed out ominously and specifically in its report, "was in the track of the *Fitzgerald.*" It was shallow enough to have torn the bottom of the Fitzgerald in storm conditions.

The *Fitzgerald* was way off course, according to testimony given at an inquiry, and few disagree. But no one ever was able to prove that the ship actually did hit Six Fathom Shoals. If it could have been proven that the *Fitz* had hit the reef, lawsuits for untold millions could have been initiated against the operators of the *Fitzgerald,* not only for the ship and cargo, but for the loss of the 29-man crew.

The *Fitzgerald* tragedy was the greatest financial loss in the history of Great Lakes sailing. She was worth nearly $24 million at the time she sank; that figure is for the ship only and does not include the loss of her 26,116 tons of taconite cargo.

The Coast Guard's extensive investigations were conducted on the wreck site itself, using a tethered, remotely operated underwater research vehicle known as an ROV, shooting 43,000 feet of videotape and taking nearly 900 photographs. But there was no *official* governmental investigation into whether the Six Fathom Shoal reef could have torn the bottom of the big ore carrier — causing the *Fitzgerald* a 15-degree list from flooding within 15 minutes of her passage.

The question arises as to what could have been identified on the "new reef" had an underwater survey been conducted the following spring after the *Fitzgerald* sank? If the actual site of the collision could have been located, the reef would have told its own story.

"You would see scrape marks, gouges in the stone, some bottom paint, rust and possibly metal scraps," Tom Farnquist told me, adding that today, years later, "everything would be gone but the metal." He concluded, "chances are that not much is left today."

Farnquist posed another question: If the *Fitzgerald* had scraped bottom on a reef, then why doesn't some track show on the aft section? True, the forward section is buried in mud, but the bottom of the 253 feet of stern section is turned upside down, and clearly visible. He pointed out that this stern section remains undented, unscratched and relatively unmarked by the teeth of a reef.

Farnquist has established a *Fitzgerald* memorial on Whitefish Point. A manned diver — the first diver ever to reach the *Fitz's* dark depths — brought back the *Fitzgerald's* bell, which is now a part of the memorial. In a public ceremony held on November 10 — the date of the *Fitzgerald's* sinking — the bell was chimed in the company of the families of the crew members of the sunken ship.

As I stood on wind-whipped Whitefish Point, I realized that no one would ever know for certain precisely what happened to the *Fitzgerald*. There were no witnesses, for the *Fitzgerald* took all her crew with her; all anyone can do now is speculate, surmise, and draw some conclusions on the possible causes of the sinking. The big lake is not letting go of its secrets — only a few clues that let us understand the tragedy more fully.

Tom Farnquist, the man who has spent more time down on the *Fitzgerald's* wreck than any other, told me bluntly: "No one will ever determine why that ship went down."

CHAPTER EIGHTEEN

WARRIORS
OF THE
STORM

As I GAZED SHOREWARD from the helm of our catamaran, I began to think about another era on the lake. What would it be like to row out from a storm-lashed shore in the dead of winter in a small wooden boat? This Shipwreck Coast was once the home of men who did just that. They were called the "warriors of the storm."

They are gone now, those gallant men in their wooden boats, but in their lifetime they were the stuff of legends and genuine folk heroes. They carved a history of life saving and rescues under extreme conditions; some of the stories of their courage and gallantry are incredible.

The prime job of the United States Life-Saving Service on Superior was to row a surfboat or lifeboat in any kind of weather, winter storms included, to rescue sailors and ships. This was often a daring and highly skilled procedure in which they launched a boat through heavy breakers. They had an unofficial motto: "You have to go out. You don't have to come back."

The first Life-Saving stations on Lake Superior opened in 1876 along the Shipwreck Coast at Vermilion Point, Crisp Point, Two Hearted River and Muskalonge Lake. The Life Saving stations are gone now with the exception of the remains of the Vermilion Point Station, now in ruins and resembling a ghost town. The Vermilion Point Station was once known as the most isolated life saving station on the big lake. It was the last rescue station available to vessels in distress until reaching Whitefish Point (when coming downbound) or the first station leaving Whitefish Point (heading upbound) on the Shipwreck Coast.

Their surfboat was a wooden 25-foot rowing vessel, lightweight for its size at 700 to 1,000 pounds. It could be hauled to the water's edge near the wreck site by Life Savers in harnesses and was used when a surf launch was necessary. The Life Saver's larger boat was the 30 to 36-foot lifeboat, weighing from two to four tons. It was primarily launched by rails directly from the Life Saving station.

Both boats were self-bailing and self-righting; any water that came in would run out, and, if overturned, the boat would right itself. Both boats were undecked and open; waves sometimes swept over the crew. The surfmen sat two abreast, in three pairs, each manning an oar, so that a surfboat was powered by six oars. The Captain was in the stern using an oar trailing behind to steer.

They were exceptional handlers of their small boats. In a storm, the Life Savers could launch their boat through the surf and row through heavy breakers to reach a stranded vessel. Though the surf launches were dangerous and difficult, their landings on storm-swept beaches were regarded as harder. This sometimes was accomplished by using a drogue — a canvas sea anchor that looked like a sort of bucket. Trailing a drogue, the steersman would attempt to hold the surfboat stern-to in the waves. However, should the boat get away from him, it could turn its beam to the waves, capsize in the heavy surf, and kill the surfmen. Many Lake Superior Life Savers were lost in capsizes.

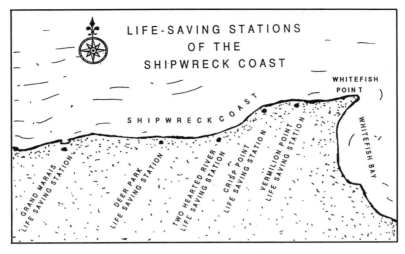

LIFE-SAVING STATIONS
OF THE
SHIPWRECK COAST

For close-in rescues, the Life Savers also could use a Lyle gun, which was mounted on a cart pulled by the men to the surf's edge. The 185-pound gun fired a line to a stranded vessel up to 600 yards away. When they had a line to the vessel, the Life Savers could rig up a breeches buoy (a life ring with a pair of canvas breeches sewn in) and haul sailors, one at a time, from a wreck.

The Live Savers had to be expert sailors and boatmen. They couldn't be younger than 18 years of age nor older than 45; they couldn't weigh fewer than 135 pounds nor more than 205. They had to live within the district of their surf station and they had to be good swimmers. Their pay for all this was $65 a month, with the Station Keeper receiving $10 more.

The station was on duty 24 hours a day, with a lookout always posted in open lookout towers. The lookout was required to ring a bell at regular intervals, primarily to prove that he was still awake. The lookout posts were without seats, so the lookout could only stand. At night, beach patrols with lanterns in hand walked along the shore, in all kinds of weather, searching for a boat being overwhelmed by a storm, a wreck coming ashore, or even debris or bodies washed up by the waves.

New recruits on beach patrol were warned to beware the ghost of Three-Fingered Riley, a seaman washed ashore during a winter storm. When the Life Savers had to chop the corpse's hand out of the ice, they slipped — and accidentally cut off two of Riley's fingers. It was said he was still looking for his missing fingers.

Today, it seems almost incredible that anyone would enter stormy Lake Superior in an open wooden boat powered only by oars. Still, stories abound about the Life Saving Service's heroism and tenacity when called into action to save lives or ships. There were many rescues made under extreme conditions by the "heroes of the surf," but certain stories of rescues on Lake Superior stand out:

The 177-foot three-masted schooner *Phineas S. Marsh* was caught August 26, 1896 in the teeth of a northwest gale off the Shipwreck Coast's Crisp Point. Leaking badly in the heavy seas, she tried to make it into the safety of Whitefish Point. Seas regularly boarded her decks; water rose in the bilges.

When the Crisp Point Station life savers saw the *Marsh's* distress flare, they launched their lifeboat through the heavy surf. It took them nearly two and a half hours to row off the shore in high waves, but as they neared the doomed schooner, the *Marsh* rolled heavily to port, then sank to the bottom, only 22 feet below. The crew managed to scramble up the masts and rigging, now at an angle because the schooner heeled to one side. Two of the crew and a cook were washed overboard. Because the spars hung over the struggling crew members, two sailors hoisted themselves into the rigging. But the cook, a woman in heavy 1890's clothing, splashed about and was unable to clamber up.

The lifeboat maneuvered under the swaying rigging and hauled the drowning cook out of the water. As the Life Savers backed their oars, several of the *Marsh's* crew in the rigging panicked and dropped into the lifeboat, injuring one of the Life Savers. The lifeboat pulled away from the wreck and landed three survivors on the beach. They then returned in two more trips to rescue the rest of the crew. None were lost.

Late in the shipping season, the surfmen had to face not only a stormy lake but also bitter cold and snow. On November 15, 1887, the *Starrucca*, a 218-foot wooden steamer, was caught in a northern gale as she headed upbound for Duluth. About 10 miles east of Grand Marais, in the midst of snow squalls and heavy waves, she drove onto a sandbar about a half mile off-shore.

The Deer Park Life Savers launched their surfboat and rowed 12 miles to the stricken *Starrucca*. When they reached her at about 5 p.m., the captain decided he'd stay until the seas became more moderate and then he'd try to save his vessel. The Life Savers rowed to the beach, setting up camp to keep watch on the grounded vessel. The storm got worse; breakers slammed over the vessel's cabins.

At midnight, the captain signaled for help and the Life Savers fought their way out from the storm-scoured shore. Freezing spray inundated them; waves regularly swept on board. They made three trips — through the surf, fighting their way to the vessel, and then returning to land in the heavy breakers — to rescue all on board.

By the time they finished, the men were frostbitten, half frozen and exhausted. The surfboat, equipment and the crew's clothing had completely iced over.

Late in October, 1887, the *Alva Bradley*, an 189-foot wooden schooner, ran aground in gale-force winds and thick snow near Marquette, Michigan. Seas 20 feet high overran her deck and tore away her yawl boat; her railings, decks, rigging and lower masts were coated with ice. Pounded against rocks by heavy waves, she was in danger of breaking up.

The Portage Lake Life Saving Station, located near the entrance of the Portage Lake Ship Canal, heard the call for help late in the afternoon. But how could Captain Albert Ocha and his crew get their surfboat nearly the 130 miles to the wreck site?

An incredible rescue began as Captain Ocha and his crew of eight rowed their boat in the storm to Houghton, Michigan. There they lashed it down on a flatcar behind a locomotive, which roared through the snow-covered countryside. When the train arrived at Marquette later that night, the Life Savers unloaded their boat and equipment onto wagons and ran them to the surf's edge. It was about 1 a.m. when they climbed in, and tethered it behind the tugboat, *A.C. Adams*, which gave them a tow into the blustering lake.

It was the worst storm of the season. In their open surfboat, the Life Savers felt the full force of the gale. The spray that coated them, their boat, and their oars quickly turned to ice.

Nearing the stranded *Bradley*, a crewman severed the frozen towline with an ax, and the Life Savers rowed desperately in the darkness toward the stranded schooner's anchor light. About an hour later, after the Life Savers fought their way into the schooner's lee, the *Bradley's* crew crawled aboard the surfboat. In the storm, the Life Savers rowed back to a rendezvous point, but, through a mixup in signals, the tugboat that would tow them had departed.

The Life Savers began to row to Marquette.

The *Bradley's* sailors, lying in the bottom of the surfboat and shivering uncontrollably from the icy water that had splashed on board, begged to return to the stricken schooner. The surfboat returned to the *Bradley* at about 4 a.m. to allow her crewmen warm up. At dawn, because the *Bradley* was in danger of breaking up, the *Bradley's* crew and the Life Savers scrambled back on board the surfboat.

This time, Captain Ocha headed toward a bonfire he could see on the beach that had been built as an all-night vigil by the townspeople. With great skill, he ran the dangerous breakers and put his surfboat safely on shore. The *Bradley's* crew members were carried to the fire, warmed and fed, and later taken through the woods to a waiting train.

The Life Savers launched their boat back into the surf and rowed out to the tugboat, which had returned at daylight. They took up the towline as the tug shouldered its way through the storm to Marquette.

When the gallant Life Savers reached the docks, they found they were frozen to their seats. They had to be chopped from the ice-crusted boat by the townspeople, and, later, their frozen clothing had to be cut away to let them out.

The station at Marquette, Michigan, came up with an innovation: a motor added to a lifeboat. The boat, powered by a Lake Shore Engine Works internal combustion engine, was launched in September, 1899. After trying out the new device in several Lake Superior storms, the Life Saving Service began converting some of its lifeboats to power.

By 1905, the service had 12 powerboats in operation, though

by modern standards, the power plant was decidedly primitive, cranky, and underpowered. Still, it gave the Life Savers more range and the ability to slug it out longer with Superior's gales to rescue crews of shipwrecks.

On December 7, 1927, the *Altadoc*, 365 feet long and upbound to Fort William, lost her steering gear in heavy seas. Helpless in the waves churned by 70-mile-an-hour gusts, and blinded by heavy snow, she and her crew of 25 drove hard ashore on the Keweenaw Point's rocks.

At Eagle Harbor, over 23 miles away, the Life Saving Station heard the stricken vessel's emergency radio transmissions and contacted their Boatswain, Anthony F. Glaza, who had been on liberty in Hancock, Michigan. Because the roads were clogged with snow, Glaza started back in the blizzard, first by streetcar, then by county snowplow and then riding in a horse-drawn sleigh. He walked the last six miles and by midnight, he was at his station.

The next day, the storm jammed the harbor with ice. Because his boat could not get out, Glaza loaded his motorized wooden surfboat on a sleigh, hired a team of horses, and pulled the boat around the bay to where he and his crew could wait for an icebreaker to cross the lake from Two Harbors, Minnesota. When the icebreaker did not arrive, the Life Savers wrestled their boat across the packed ice field until they could splash it into the waves. The effort took them about five hours.

Plunging through heavy seas for about two and a half hours, they came alongside the wrecked freighter. Two of the Life Saving crew went on board and 14 of the ship's crew made their way down into the ice-coated surfboat. Glaza turned his helm for Copper Harbor and, a little after 3 p.m., put the *Altadoc's* crew on shore.

The storm grew worse; the temperature was dropping. Glaza put a canvas cover over part of the boat as the Life Savers fought their way back to the stricken vessel to pick up the remainder of the crew, their luggage, and the Life Savers' own two men.

Returning to Copper Harbor at about 6:30 that evening, the motorized surfboat became iced in. To free it, the weary, frostbitten Life Savers rocked the boat in the inch-and-a-half thick ice. Water sloshed onto the engine; it stopped. They were powerless and stranded in a field of ice.

A searchlight shone from the distance. It was the Coast Guard cutter *Crawford*, which had finally made its way across Superior, despite 27 degrees below zero cold. It cut a path through the ice to the surfboat and took the Life Savers and the *Altadoc* crew on board.

The next morning, the *Crawford* left for Eagle Harbor, towing the surfboat behind. Entering the harbor, she began to cut through the thick ice, but damaged both propellers.

Undaunted, the Life Savers dropped onto the ice and man-handled their iced-up surfboat back to their station.

They found four planks cracked and the boat's sides cut by the ice, but the gallant little boat had won — not a single man was lost to Superior.

To me, the Storm Warriors have carved out one of the most heroic and notable sagas of humanity against Superior.

As we sailed past the desolate places where Superior's first life saving stations once stood, I took off my cap in silent tribute.

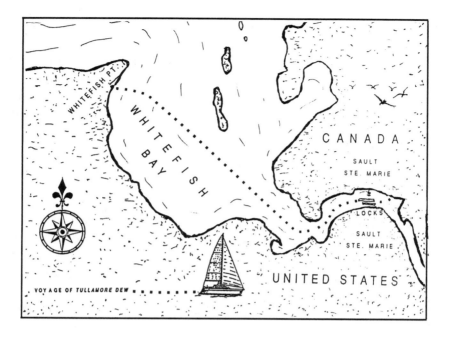

CHAPTER NINETEEN

TO THE
RENDEZVOUS

IT WAS A GLORIOUS DAY to be sailing across Whitefish Bay. In the distance, I could see the blue-gray loom of the Canadian shore of the great lake as it narrowed to its easternmost point. We were on the final leg of our downbound voyage, headed for the historic "Soo."

The "Soo" is Sault Ste Marie, so named because of its rapids ("Sault" in French) — a mile of raging white water. Two cities are split by the St. Mary's river, one on the Canadian side and the other on the U.S. side. We were heading for the Great Lakes Cruising Club Rendezvous on the Canadian side.

Today we had a beautiful sailing day, with bright and sunny skies and winds out of the northwest at 7 to 10 knots. We had left Whitefish Harbor at about 8 a.m. and were now sailing in the company of the 37-foot sloop, *Katy*.

It was not long before Joe and Thom were on the bow, hauling up a large nylon sail bag from the forward bow locker, and unfolding a voluminous sail. Joe was finally going to fly his big chute.

They spent several minutes tying on lines, and then, with Bruce grinding away on the winches, the chute was up and blossoming hugely over the bow. As it tugged at our boat, I took over the helm. It was my first experience behind a big spinnaker and it hauled us along beautifully. Picking up speed, we were soon cruising past *Katy*.

We began to see ocean-going vessels as well as giant thousand-foot-long ore boats. We'd be coming close to them as we entered the locks, a new experience for me. When we were near the entry, we dropped the spinnaker and began to motor through carefully marked deep-water channels, which we now shared with the huge steel ships.

Ahead lay one of the busiest canal systems in the world, with giant ships of all flags passing up and down the St. Mary's river. Here the locks carry twice the traffic of the Panama Canal — mostly ocean-going salt-water freighters and large ore carriers — and, today, us.

We'd pass through the U.S. locks, the last of 16 water steps in the Great Lakes-St. Lawrence Seaway system, which connects Lake Superior to the Atlantic Ocean more than 2,000 miles away.

As we cruised along under diesel power, I took a moment to appreciate some of the history of the Sault and the locks. Where I gazed toward shore, dwellings of Native American villages had stood proudly, for the Sault was once held sacred in Ojibway mythology.

This was the traditional meeting place for the tribes to gather each spring and fall to harvest whitefish runs on the river's rapids. They called it "Bawating," which meant, "water pitching over rock," because Superior discharged itself through a narrow outlet descending about 20 feet over a ledge of sandstone studded with granite boulders.

Here the largest surface body of fresh water in the world was "discovered" by Europeans. Since about the early 1600s, the Sault became a launching site for explorers, adventurers, voyageurs, black robes, sailors, and all who traveled into mighty Superior.

In about 1620, the shadowy figure of Etienne Brule, the first white man to explore Superior, passed through here — he was about 30 years old, but already worn and aged from his rough life and tortures at the hands of the Iroquois. Jean Nicolet came through in 1634; Radisson and Groseilliers in 1656, and in the 1660's came the first black robe, Father Jacques Marquette, who founded the first Jesuit mission in what is now Michigan.

As the last point of civilization before jumping off into the wilderness, the Sault must have presented an unusual picture. In 1839, Mrs. Anna Jameson, a visiting Englishwoman, described the Sault's two sides. The United States side, she wrote, had an "unmilitary looking" garrison and a fortress of cedar posts, but, alas, the Canadian side did not have "even these demonstrations of power or prosperity."

She wrote that close by the United States fort there was a small factory belonging to the North-West Fur Company and below this, "a few miserable log-huts, occupied by some French Canadians and voyageurs in the service of the company, a set of lawless mauvais sujets, from all I can learn. Lower down stands the house of Mr. and Mrs. MacMurray, with the Chippewa village under their care and tuition, but most of the wigwams and their inhabitants are now on their way down the lake. A lofty eminence, partly cleared and partly clothed with forest, rises behind the house on which stand the little mission- ary church and the schoolhouse...From the summit of this hill you look over the traverse into Lake Superior and the two giant capes which guard its entrance."

The area saw its share of violence. A fort located along the canal was the site of a massacre during the French regime. This was also where the British North West Company located on the United States side in the late 1700's. In the War of 1812, the British fur trading post was burned by the United States Army.

The Sault was also once the home of author Henry Schoolcraft, the U.S. Indian Agent who became an authority on Native Americans. It was Schoolcraft's tales of Indian legends around Superior that caught the eye of poet Longfellow, and resulted in the famous poem, *The Song of Hiawatha*.

Somewhere along the canal, in the old district of the Sault, was Schoolcraft's original house.

Father Claude Dablon in 1669-70 described the rapids of St. Mary's River, which ran nearly a mile and dropped about 21 feet, as "A very violent current of waters from Lake Superior...checked by a great number of rocks...(forming) a dangerous cascade of half a league in width, all these waters descending and plunging headlong together, as by the flight of stairs, over the rocks which bar the whole river."

In the early days, Frenchmen coming through the area would simply portage their birch-bark canoes around the turbulent rapids. The first rudimentary canal was built in 1789 by the North West Fur Company. It was several thousand feet long and eight feet wide — big enough for the canoes and boats of the day to get around the mile of white water.

The "modern" lock and canal system, built in 1855, has been repeatedly enlarged and improved. But I had to smile a little at the controversy that erupted in 1852 when the U.S. Congress was asked to approve money for this ship canal. One Senator rose during the debate to argue that to build a canal at the Sault was "work beyond the remotest settlement of the United States, if not the moon."

The locks were completed in time to carry the fabulous iron and copper discoveries of northern Michigan to a world market. Later, thanks to the canal, the even larger iron ore strikes in Minnesota would turn Superior into the world's largest supplier of iron ore.

The most recent U.S.-built lock was completed in 1969, the only lock large enough to accommodate today's 1,000-foot super lakers.

For our catamaran, cruising into the lock area was like being on a well-marked highway. We had charts of the area and there were ample signs to tell us where to go. We glided close to the huge steel salties and super lakers. From our vantage point, they seemed as immense as a skyscraper turned over on its side, but somehow able to float and move.

A green signal — and we motored into the lock. Inside was a huge concrete cavern, dripping with moss and algae. I looked up to see the blue sky. We had put fenders along the side of our hull to hold us away from the concrete locks; a lock worker threw down several long ropes. I was ready at the bow with

Bruce and we grabbed the line as it fell to the deck. Behind us, huge doors closed.

Water rushed in. We hung onto the rope in the swirling water, holding the big cat in position along the lock wall. Slowly, we were elevated toward the sky.

Then we were up at the top of the lock, and it seemed to me we had suddenly burst into civilization. People were everywhere, with grinning faces. Gaily colored flags fluttered. I saw several children waving at us; I waved back. They waved all the harder, with their accompanying adults pointing at us and then joining in. I saw that the spectators were on an observation platform set back from the canal itself and busy watching boats, including ours, coming through the locks. There was an unexpected air of festivity about the place.

"Do you see the golden building?" Someone was on the VHF, giving us directions over the radio.

We turned north, heading toward a golden building that turned out to be the Canadian side's City Hall. I saw a beautiful new marina overshadowed by what looked to be a huge tent. This was the Tent Pavilion, which soared nearly 100 feet high, and was part of a waterfront park. Off to our right, on the water's edge, was the Ontario Bush Plane Heritage and Forest Fire Educational Center.

We were told to enter McLean Harbor, alongside the golden building. That turned out to be a small harbor slip, big enough for us to enter with caution. I was on the bow watching the water of the harbor grow shallower. Down below, I could see rocks.

Ahead, past a row of cruising keelboats, I saw a spidery-looking catamaran snugged into the very end. We came in alongside to "raft up", tying our boat to the other cat.

Bruce walked over the other boat and from shore threw lines to Thom and me. We secured our cat as we floated lightly atop what looked like five or six feet of water. We had arrived.

Little by little, the stress and tension of the voyage seemed to lift. Here we were, in this picturesque Canadian harbor, a very interesting catamaran alongside us, and a grove of trees to the other side, shading our little patch of water. Birds seemed to sing a welcome.

I decided to get ashore and explore. I gingerly made my way across the tethered catamaran to pier's side, then walked north past the golden building toward a swooping series of concrete harbors and piers.

The Canadian marina, I saw, was filled with cruising boats of all sizes and types, glistening in the sun, neatly aligned in their slips or carefully tied up to one another. Flags flew from mast tops, along the running backstays, and from varnished transoms. There were many sailboats, ketches, sloops and cutters, most of fiberglass construction but a few of wood; some trawler-type vessels, and some large power cruisers.

They were part of the Great Lakes Cruising Club at its Diamond Jubilee Rendezvous. At the hospitality building, several friendly people gave me a name tag, with a ribbon showing that I was at my first rendezvous. The club has been holding them since 1934.

It was a great pleasure for me to see all the assembled cruising boats. I seldom meet a boat I don't like, and as I began talking with others at the Rendezvous, I realized I was with kindred spirits. We talked of sailing Superior, of storms, of making passage in rough weather, and specifically, of crossing the big lake for the meeting here.

As I walked back to our harbor, though, I could not shake off a sense of nostalgia. Strolling along the modern concrete walkways, I thought about the history that these shores had seen.

Here the voyageurs had assembled their birch-bark canoes before they headed across Superior into the wilderness. Here, too, the black robes had strolled before they left the last trace of civilization to face privation and even death in the north woods. All would be following the watery trail that I had just come across. As I gazed westward, I wondered what their thoughts might have been.

After I returned, I saw that the owners were coming on board the catamaran next to us. This was a vessel much lower to the water than our Island Packet Cat; it had an almost spidery look to it with its smaller hulls and sleek cabin. I looked closer: its light gray color was worn in places and weathered. But there was something else that I sensed: the cat exuded something unidentifiable, as if it had just come through some long-distance cruising.

Lyle Burke hoisted himself out of his electric scooter onto the cockpit. "I've got the hand holds memorized," he said cheerfully as he came on board with wife, Nancy.

He invited me to join them and I carefully stepped down from *Tullamore Dew* onto the little gray cruising cat and moved into a low cockpit topped with a permanent bimini top. Lyle explained that he had multiple sclerosis (MS) and that he could not walk except short distances with the aid of arm crutches.

On land, he uses his motorized four-wheel scooter, but on the catamaran he said he can move about with ease, except that he has difficulty going forward to the bow because the cat has narrow side decks.

As we talked, I learned that he, Nancy, and their ship's cat Ming were from Duluth, Minnesota, and had recently completed a 7,000-mile cruise.

Their catamaran, named *Sam*, is an English-built Iroquois MK2a model with an extended stern, differentiating it from the other Iroquois cats which were designed to be cruiser/racers. Lyle's and Nancy's cat was 31 1/2 feet in length with a width of 13 1/2 feet. Built in 1978, *Sam* weighed, unloaded, about 6,800 pounds — a very light boat.

"I looked for what I really needed," Lyle said. After his condition was diagnosed as MS, he found himself having a harder time getting around a sailboat. He and Nancy used to sail a trimaran, but he said that was like a "skinny monohull," with lots of up and down clambering required on the boat.

"My balance was not so good," he explained, so they looked for a sailboat that would be easier for him to get around in and also more stable. That meant a catamaran. They narrowed their choices down to the Iroquois MK2 and found five to look at, with all but one boat in Florida. The MK2a, with the extended stern, was the cat they really liked. Lyle said, "It was not a spur of the moment decision."

I could see why they chose the design. Though low, the cockpit was quite large. Two wooden tillers extended forward from the transoms, linked together by an aluminum bar. Between the two hulls hung a small outboard engine, with controls leading to the cockpit. I looked above me and saw additional hand-holds in the semi-permanent top covering the cockpit. This was a good station from which to operate a boat in all weather, and, with additional handholds, I could see how Lyle could move around the cockpit with agility during their long cruises.

After they purchased her, Nancy and Lyle had the cat truck-ed from Florida to Duluth's Park Point, where they also had their home. They tested their boat on Lake Superior, and, find-ing they truly enjoyed the boat, they gradually extended their cruises from several days to several weeks. After Lyle retired, they tried a six-week cruise. It was successful — now they were ready for a longer voyage.

In the fall of 1990, they had their catamaran trucked south from Duluth to Afton, Minnesota, put their boat in the St. Croix River and hoisted their mast. It was the start of a year-long sail-ing odyssey that carried them to Florida and the Bahamas, up the Atlantic Coast, and finally, back to Duluth — a total of about 7,000 miles.

To begin, they cruised downstream to the Mississippi River and then branched into the Ohio River. They followed the Ten-nessee River until they came onto the Tom Bigbee (Tenn-Tom) Waterway, which they followed through Mississippi and Alabama. Entering the Gulf of Mexico, they headed eastward and "hopped along" the east coast of Florida to spend a sunny Christmas in Naples. They sailed to the Dry Tortugas and then to the Bahamas for about two months.

There they broke a rudder. "It just snapped right off," Lyle said. Limping into a harbor on Eleuthera Island in the Bahamas, the cruising couple made a temporary repair, which held for a while; they crossed the Gulf Stream to Key Largo on one rudder. Lyle rationalized, "monohulls cross the Stream on just one rudder. Why not us?"

At Key Largo, Lyle found a "palm-tree carpenter" who "literally built us two new rudders in the shade of a palm tree." Sam's new rudders were constructed of two 3/4-inch thick marine plywood sheets, epoxied together into a strong inch-and-a-half-thick rudder, then faired and covered with fiberglass.

They sailed up the East Coast, staying on the ocean until they were north of Miami and could enter the Intercostal Waterway, where it was "easy going" until they came to Chesapeake Bay. They re-entered the Atlantic and came into New York's harbor.

"We took the tide through New York," Lyle said. "We zoomed through Manhattan in about an hour." They unstepped the mast for the first time since they left Minnesota to enter the Erie Canal. They motored to Oswego, New York, crossed Lake Ontario, and, via Canada's Trent-Severn Waterway, ended up in Lake Huron's Georgian Bay. From there they entered the Sault locks, and crossed Lake Superior to return to Duluth.

"The scariest thing on the whole trip was once when we nearly ran aground," Lyle said. He explained that they used an automatic helm the entire trip, correcting their course with a hand-held remote control, so they could be fairly relaxed. As Lyle explained, he and Nancy are inveterate readers and "always have a book in their hands."

All of a sudden, as they were cruising leisurely, Nancy looked up and asked, "Where are you going?" Lyle glanced up from his book. They were headed for shore.

The catamaran brushed the bank before Lyle could steer away. What had happened, he explained, was that because he had forgotten to turn off the automatic pilot when passing beneath it, a bridge's magnetism had thrown off the steering. "We had grass stains on the boat," he mused.

Windy conditions and storms don't much bother the Burkes. "We get used to it," Lyle explained. "The cat doesn't pitch; if we are going into the waves, the hulls pierce the waves and pop up. It's an abrupt movement, but they do float up, as opposed to the yawing of a monohull. It's a surprisingly dry ride."

He explained that they prefer multihull cruising because "the more wind you get, the faster the cat wants to sail. What you do is reduce sail until you are comfortable. You point fairly well; downwind in Superior's waves is deceptively friendly. If it's blowing all that much, then all you've got up is part of a jib. You run steadily and don't thrash side to side. Being on a downwind run is a little like being on a railroad track. "

"We've been in some pretty rough stuff, but we're on autopilot all the way. Once, coming into the Superior entryway, we had a northeaster blowing and high waves. A number of big freighters were anchored off the entryway, waiting to enter. When our cat went down in a trough and I stood in the cockpit, we were down deep enough that the 60 to 70-foot-high freighters would be lost from sight."

He explained that because they had to be at work on Monday, "We just rode the northeaster in. It was not a scary ride, but under sail you have to be careful."

As experienced Superior sailors, Lyle and Nancy keep a constant eye out for a weather front. He said, "You can see it coming from the northwest. And you can feel the dead calm preceding it. Then it's time to get out of there."

"If we don't have a dying need to go out, we don't go out," Lyle explained. "We pay a lot of attention to weather. If it turns foggy, we turn around and go back to port. If it's not fun, why do it?"

The catamaran is powered by a 10-horsepower, four-stroke outboard Yamaha with a long shaft; the Burkes used it throughout the 7,000-mile cruise when there was no wind. Lyle showed me how easy it was to lower the engine's drive shaft via a swinging bracket into the water. A push of an electric button started the two-cylinder engine; remote controls let Lyle control the throttle and shift gears. Typically, the Burkes cruise their cat under power at around 5 1/4 knots "for reasons of economy."

I worked the tiller bar to see how easily the cat steered. Lyle was showing me the automatic pilot and the engine controls when my eye was caught by a small furry creature in the cabin. "That's Ming," Nancy explained. "We have a ship's cat on board and she is Siamese."

Ming cruises everywhere with the Burkes but apparently has her own views of strangers. She disappeared from sight when I went below with Nancy and Lyle. Inside the streamlined cabin, the Iroquois had standing room near the cockpit, but forward and to the sides, the area narrowed to somewhat less than full headroom. It was comfortable and wide, though.

As I seated myself, Ming came over to me. She was a beautiful three-year-old seal point. "We don't keep her below," Lyle explained. "She chooses to be below. If we are underway, she finds a comfortable place. When we dock, she comes out."

"She gets shore leave, of course," Lyle said with a grin.

Everything has its place in the cruising catamaran. There were bunks, some of which were filled with gear; there was a galley and a head. I wondered where the vessel carried the electric scooter that Lyle used for his shore excursions. There seemed to be no place to put it.

"It comes apart in sections," Lye explained. "The batteries and the rear drive go in the starboard stern compartment; the basket and cowling go in the spare bunk; the front unit and wheels are stored in a forward compartment. It takes about five minutes to disassemble." I admired Lyle's ingenuity.

"We've spent more time sailing since I was diagnosed with MS than before," he said. "We savor our time on the water a little more; the only thing MS has forced me to do is bring a crew: I can't stand on the foredeck, for example, and anchor. I can't get off the deck with dock line to tie up. For that, I need crew." Lyle's crew, of course, was Nancy.

As I left Lyle and Nancy, I wondered at the name they had given their boat. "It's named after our deceased cat, Sam," Lyle explained. "He was with us for 15 years and he was a very unusual and unique cat. He died the year before we got this boat. We thought it would be great to have our new cat named after our last cat."

CHAPTER TWENTY

HOMEWARD
BOUND

THE JULY SUN was a teaser, a layer of brilliant sunshine and warmth inserted between rain, fog and chill. It would not hold, I knew, for the weather forecast already told me that another low was whipping our way. I could feel the unsettled weather creeping up through my well-worn deck shoes. I raised my face to the wind and took a deep, sweet breath of the lake-burnished air.

There was something else that bothered me.

My voyage was completed. It was time for me to leave Lake Superior.

Getting out of the Sault turned out to be more of a problem than getting in. We were, in effect, in the middle of nowhere so far as commercial land transportation was concerned. There were no airline flights back to Bayfield, Wisconsin, where Thom's car was parked. Nor a train, nor a bus.

The only way out for us was to take a van from the Sault to St. Ignace, Michigan, where we could pick up an overnight bus ride to Ashland, Wisconsin. We didn't know how we'd get to Bayfield, about 20 miles beyond Ashland.

Thom Burns left the boat to check into arrangements while Joe and I began to clean up *Tullamore Dew* after our journey. We started on the bow with cleaning mops and buckets and worked all the way aft, washing and polishing the hull topsides. Actually, I enjoyed that job, working out on deck in the fresh air and sunshine. It wouldn't last long.

That morning, I had packed my bags and gear for the long trip home. Because I knew that I'd have to lug a lot of stuff by hand, and I had a number of parcels with me by now — my sea bag, my camera gear, my foul weather gear and boots, plus several presents for my family back home — I realized I couldn't carry everything.

I had, however, a big roll of duct tape from my boat that I had lent Joe, and the solution seemed obvious: I duct taped everything together. The bags, boots, and packages were swathed in silver ribbons and the whole assemblage looked make-shift. I caught a few knowing looks from the crew. But at least I could now carry all my belongings.

Suddenly, I saw Thom walking rapidly toward the slip. "We've got to leave — now!" he announced.

I jumped into a dry set of jeans, stuck my feet back into my wet deck shoes, added a last bit of duct tape to my bulging bags, and exited *Tullamore Dew* by way of walking over *Sam*, the catamaran.

There we encountered our first problem: how to get ourselves and our gear out of the harbor to where we could find a taxi. I stood in a parking lot, bags beside me when I saw a van driving slowly by. I signalled to it and a friendly Canadian face peered out: he was at the marina to look at the boats. We needed a lift to a taxi stand? No problem. Minutes later, we were at a hotel. We called for a cab and shortly one arrived.

"We want to go to the van office on the American side," Thom said.

I glanced at my watch: we had about a half hour to go. I asked, "How much?"

"Twenty six bucks," the driver said.

I coughed; that was a lot of money for a drive of maybe five or six miles, from one side of the river to the other. But we were behind on our schedule. There was one van out of here, the only one connecting with a solitary bus that would take us back. Otherwise we'd wait days for the next bus.

Neither Thom nor I had twenty six dollars Canadian. I asked if the driver would take United States currency.

"Even up," he said. The U.S. dollar was worth about a third more than the Canadian dollar, which meant that we were being taken for a ride, in more ways than one.

But did we have a choice? I checked my watch again: we were running late.

Our wallets lighter, we drove hurriedly out of the Canadian side of Sault Ste. Marie and headed out over the long bridge connecting the two nations. On the other side of the concrete span were lines of cars stretched back miles.

The driver felt talkative: "Canadian customs has been tightening up. Those cars'll be searched for American goods that Canadians need to pay tax on." I looked out over the rows of cars: they faced an hour's wait, perhaps more, at the Canadian border.

It occurred to me that the taxi driver would also be stuck in that jam, and I lightened up. Maybe he'd actually earn his exorbitant fee.

On the way to the U.S. side, we passed right through customs. But soon it was clear that the driver did not know where to go. We gave him a street name, and he finally stopped to ask someone for directions. We made our way toward the edge of town, and ahead was a motel office. An office clerk came out to book us on the van ride.

"How soon?" I asked.

"About 4 or 5 minutes," he said.

"You time these things a little close," I said to Thom.

Soon the van arrived, and we wound around the hills as dusk fell. When we left the main highway, and I began to worry about our bus connection, the driver told us that he had another fare to pick up. We entered a fenced-in area where two large men waited with a younger man between them, a scruffy-looking suitcase by his side. We had stopped at a correctional institute; our van, now complete with former inmate, was on its way again down the tip of Michigan on Hwy. 75.

On our left, we could see the winking lights of Lake Huron, and signs announcing the Mackinac Island ferry. Another left, along the windy roads, and we saw the big waters of Lake Michigan.

It was dark when we arrived at St. Ignace; the van driver cautioned, "The bus will be here any minute."

I carried my bags into what the driver said was the bus station, and I glanced about. The building might have passed for a hallway in better times. It was an old, short, narrow room, with several wooden benches, a couple of beat-up coin-operated entertainment machines that no one was using, and a ticket cage that was shuttered up and locked tight.

And, I quickly determined, no rest rooms.

I wanted to rest. This was getting to be a land voyage from Hades. Perhaps I had grown soft on our catamaran on Lake Superior, I thought to myself. I wiped the sweat from my face with the back of my sweaty hand. I'd just have to adjust; still, one had certain physical needs.

Checking around, I saw that across the street was a bar. Bars served beer, I reckoned, and where there were beer drinkers there were bound to be rest rooms. Ah, the benefits of a liberal arts education.

"The bus will be here any minute," Thom said, worried. Still, I felt a higher priority, so to speak, and I left my bags with Thom to guard, along with the released prisoner. A light rain began to fall on me as I walked across the road to the bar.

Minutes after I returned, the bus arrived. We boarded it and Thom took the seats ahead of me, wedged his jacket to one side, and slumped, attempting to relax.

I wished him luck as I spread myself out in my row of seats, but the seats were hard, with the top where my head rested made of a metal bar. I wedged in my foul weather jacket and thought dark thoughts about the bus's designer. As we jolted down the rough Michigan secondary road, heading west on Hwy. 2, I realized it would be a long, nearly sleepless night.

Lights of towns flicked by as we skirted Lake Michigan and the Hiawatha National Forest. Below us lay the big vista of Green Bay and, across it, the Door County Peninsula. We followed the border of Michigan and Wisconsin to the north and west, coming nearer Lake Superior.

It was 5:30 a.m. when we arrived in Ashland, Wisconsin, and faced our next problem.

"How can we get to Bayfield?" I asked the driver. He hedged a bit. Actually, there wasn't a bus terminal here, only a parking lot we were getting out on. He suggested that if we walked a few blocks to a restaurant maybe we could check out some sort of bus schedule there. Maybe.

He didn't really know, but we unloaded our bags, and stood there in the parking lot, perplexed, trying to figure out what to do.

A well-dressed woman who had just entered the bus shook her gray head in sympathy. She inquired politely, "Where are you going?"

"Bayfield," I said. "Actually, Port Superior, this side of Bayfield."

"I know where *that* is," she said.

She stood up from her bus seat, then hollered: "Tom, *you* take them to Port Superior."

As if to emphasize her point, she stamped her foot.

Outside the bus, a tall gray-haired man seemed to understand. He straightened up, gave his wife a nod, then motioned to us with a little wave of his hand.

"Good thing he has a wife," she said.

Once correctly oriented, Tom turned out to be a genial host. We chatted as we drove along the windy, wooded stretch of road. He and his wife were retired and lived near Bayfield. She was on her way to Milwaukee to do some shopping and to see a play.

And, yes, he emphasized, he really was happy to help us out.

He was a sailing fan, it turned out, and was interested in our voyage across the lake. Moreover, when he found out that Thom and I were from the Twin Cities of Minneapolis and St. Paul, he remembered reading a book that was special to him.

"Schoolteacher from your area," Tom explained, "built himself a plywood boat some years back and did some sailing in it."

"Ten foot *Yankee Girl*," I offered. "Quite a boat. Set a couple of world records."

"That's right," Tom allowed. "Heck of a book, too."

"Was the name, *Alone Against the Atlantic*?" I offered.

Tom was surprised. "You read the book?"

"Oh, yes," I said. "Several times."

He part way turned around in his driver's seat, speechless for a moment, and pleased. Then we began a happy exchange of information about the book and he ended up taking us directly to beautiful Port Superior, where Thom's car was parked and where my own *Persistence* was moored along the bulkhead. We thanked him for his kindness.

After that, it was a matter of loading up the car, checking to see that my boat had been OK in my absence, and then heading south to the Twin Cities.

My sailing adventure was over, for now, and my business life — put on hold for a short time — had to be resumed. I almost cringed as I thought of deadlines and pressures. And the piles of paper on my editorial desk.

Hours later, we pulled into my driveway in Shoreview, Minnesota, where Loris and our son, Will, were waiting. "Welcome home," they greeted me.

The late morning was beautiful, golden with sunshine and a fresh land breeze. We stretched our legs, walking through the patio door into our back yard, where Loris's flowers were in full bloom; across the way a neighbor's flower garden spilled its fragrances our way.

It was a fitting welcome, at last, back to land.

Tom bade farewell, and I waved him goodbye, standing by the door with Loris as he drove off.

My long voyage was over. I was glad to be home.

Later, as I sat at my desk amid piles of paper, I had a hard time concentrating on my work.

A fresh breeze blew in the window. It seemed to be from the north.

My thoughts could not help but return to the Big Lake.

Images flashed in my mind — clean, open spaces, incredible miles of fresh water, small islands and colorful waterfront characters.

My thoughts began to stir again.

There is still something else calling me: the third leg of Superior. It lies on the Canadian side: the haunted north shore.

I wondered when I'd begin my next voyage.

ACKNOWLEDGEMENTS

A book such as this could not have been written without help from a number of people.

My special thanks to Scott Anfinson, Archeologist for the Minnesota Shipwreck Archaeology Program at the Minnesota Historical Society, Saint Paul, Minnesota, for his knowledge of sunken vessels on Superior and particularly his appreciation of the plight of what is left of the *U.S.S. Essex*, Minnesota's sloop of war.

Thanks also to David Cooper, Underwater Archeologist at the State Historical Society of Wisconsin for his underwater detective work shedding new light on the mystery of the sinking of the *Lucerne*. I also want to thank Mr. Cooper for sharing his knowledge of the *Pretoria*.

At the Canal Park Marine Museum, Duluth, Minnesota, I am deeply indebted to C. Patrick Labadie, Director and Maritime Historian, and Thomas R. Holden, Assistant Curator, for their cheerful help and expert shipwreck counsel. I especially appreciate their contributions to the chapters on the sinking of the *Edmund Fitzgerald* and on the historical aspects of Chapter Seven, *Hunters of Lost Ships*.

Thanks to Thomas L. Farnquist, President of the Great Lakes Shipwreck Historical Society, Sault Ste. Marie, Michigan, for his contributions to this book, including his insights into the mystery of the sinking of the *Edmund Fitzgerald* and for his first-hand knowledge of Superior's Shipwreck Coast.

Thanks also to Pete Conlin, Curator of the Heritage Hjemkomst Interpretive Center, Moorhead, Minnesota, for his help on *The Long Voyage of the Homecoming Ship*.

Thanks to Dr. Tom Allen, Biology Department, Lake Superior State University, Sault Ste. Marie, Michigan, under whose jurisdiction lies the last remaining Life Saving Station at Vermilion Point. His knowledge was especially helpful to me in writing *Warriors of the Storm*.

For his early-on reading of several chapters, I am grateful for the literary acumen and editorial expertise of author and agent Brian Richard Boylan, Minneapolis, Minnesota.

Special thanks are due to Joe Boland, Bruce Boland, and Thom Burns, my shipmates on the *Tullamore Dew*. A good ship and a voyage have a way of pulling people together. I deeply appreciated their companionship and general good cheer, even when Superior was at its worst.

My thanks to Dave Nixon, Chartermaster of Port Superior Charters, Bayfield, Wisconsin, for his many kindnesses during my voyages and for sharing some of his hard-won wisdom about the big lake.

Thanks also to the Reverend Curtis and Ruth Johnson, Bayfield, Wisconsin, my friends from the waterfront at Cornucopia, for their insights and inspiration over the years.

Thanks to Captain Geoff Pope, of Excelsior, Minnesota, whose fine topsail ketch the *Sheila Yeates* once graced Superior and is greatly missed, and to Bill Ferraro, of the National Park Service's Visitor Center, Bayfield, Wisconsin.

I am especially grateful to my family, Loris and Will Bree, for their support during my voyages. Without their help, I would never have been able to turn my dreams into reality — or write another book about Superior.

Thanks also to Mary Strasma, intrepid editor, for her fine hand and counsel in the final development and editing of this book.

Lastly, I want to thank the many sailors and waterfront people I've met over the years in person and through their writings who have shared so many of their insights and adventures. Sometimes, through the mists of time, we catch snatches of their visions and share their dreams. And in the process, if we are lucky, we sometimes encounter a part of ourselves.

BIBLIOGRAPHY

Bogue, Margaret Beattie and Palmer, Virginia A. *Around the Shores of Lake Superior: A Guide to Historic Sites*. Madison, WI: The University of Wisconsin Sea Grant College Program, 1979.

Bowen, Dana Thomas. *Memories of the Lakes*. Cleveland, OH: Freshwater Press, 1984.

Bree, Marlin. *In the Teeth of the Northeaster: A Solo Voyage on Lake Superior*. Hardcover edition, New York: Clarkson N. Potter, 1988. Trade paperback edition, St. Paul, MN: Marlor Press, 1993.

Canfield, Edward J. and Allan, Thomas A. *Life On a Lonely Shore: A History of the Vermilion Point Life-Saving Station*. Sault Ste. Marie, MI: Lake Superior State University Press, 1991.

Cantor, George. *The Great Lakes Guidebook*. Ann Arbor, MI: The University of Michigan Press, 1980.

Cooper, David J. and Jensen, John O. *Davidson's Goliaths: Underwater Archeological Investigations of the Steamer Frank O'Connor and the Schooner-Barge Pretoria*. Madison, WI: State Underwater Archeology Program, Division of Historic Preservation, State Historical Society of Wisconsin, 1995.

Dahl, Bonnie. *The Superior Way: A Cruising Guide to Lake Superior*. Duluth, MN: Lake Superior Port Cities, 1992.

Engman, Elmer. *Shipwreck Guide to the Western Half of Lake Superior*. Duluth, MN: Innerspace, 1976.

Hemming, Robert J. *Gales of November: The Sinking of the Edmund Fitzgerald*. Chicago, IL: Contemporary Books, 1981.

Judziewicz, Emmet J. and Koch, Rudy G. *Flora of the Apostle Is-

lands. Madison, WI: The Michigan Botanist, University of Wisconsin, 1993.

Keller, James M. *The Unholy Apostles: Shipwreck Tales of the Apostle Islands*. Bayfield, WI: Apostle Island Press, 1993.

Kohl, Johann Georg. *Kitchi-Gami: Life Among the Lake Superior Ojibway*. London: Chapman and Hall, 1860. St. Paul, MN: trade paperback reprint, the Minnesota Historical Society Press, 1985.

Lund, Dr. Duane R. *The North Shore of Lake Superior: Yesterday and Today*. Cambridge, MN: Adventure Publications, 1993.

Michigan National Resources Magazine. A *Most Superior Land, Life in the Upper Peninsula of Michigan*. Lansing, MI, 1983.

Nute, Grace Lee. *Lake Superior*. New York: Bobbs-Merrill, 1944.

Radisson, Pierre Esprit. *Explorations of Pierre Esprit Radisson*. Reprinted from the original manuscript in the British Museum. Minneapolis, MN: Ross and Haines, 1961.

Schoolcraft, Henry R. *The Hiawatha Legends*. AuTrain, MI: Avery Color Studios, 1985.

Stonehouse, Frederick. *Wreck Ashore: The United States Life-Saving Service on the Great Lakes*. Duluth, MN: Lake Superior Port Cities, 1992.

Stonehouse, Frederick. *Went Missing*. Au Train, MI: Avery Color Studies, 1984.

Stonehouse, Frederick. *Lake Superior's Shipwreck Coast: Maritime Accidents from Whitefish Bay to Grand Marais, Michigan*. Au Train, MI: Avery Color Studies, 1991.

Stonehouse, Frederick. *The Wreck of the Edmund Fitzgerald*. Au Train, MI: Avery Color Studies, 1977.

Stonehouse, Frederick. *Munising Shipwrecks*. Au Train, MI: Avery Color Studies, 1986.

Strzok, Dave. *A Visitor's Guide to the Apostle Islands National Lakeshore*. Ashland, WI: Superior Printing and Specialties, 1981.

Strzok, Dave. *Exploring Wisconsin's North Coast*. Washburn, WI: Printing Plus, 1992.

Wolff Jr., Julius F. *Lake Superior Shipwrecks: Complete Reference to Maritime Accidents and Disasters*. Duluth, MN: Lake Superior Port Cities, 1990.

PERSISTENCE

Anatomy of a small sailboat

Length overall: 20 feet
Beam: 7 foot 4 inches
Draft: Centerboard up, 12 inches
  Centerboard down, 4 feet, 6 inches
Sail area: Main, 80 square feet
  Jib, 88 square feet
Sail handling: Main has two reefing
  points, and is fully battened. Jib is set on
  furler, with controls leading to cockpit.
Construction Details:
  Keel & stem: white oak; **Stringers:**
  Sitka Spruce; **Ribs:** Mahogany composite
  Hull: three layers of 1/8-inch Western
  Red Cedar, epoxy glued and covered
  with 6-ounce fiberglass. **Bottom:**
  Additional coverings of fiberglass, with
  outer coating of epoxy and carbon
  Finishing: Hull topside is bright finished
  with UV-resistant varnish; bottom has
  anti-fouling paint.
Electrical:
  Two solar panels atop cabin recharge two
  deep cycle, 115-amp, 12-volt marine bat-
  teries under forward bunk.
Engine:
  5-horsepower Nissan outboard, mounted
  on swing bracket
Radios:
  Ham-band radio, UHF radio, AM/FM radio
Berths:
  Double berth located in forecastle; two
  quarterberths with storage underneath.
Miscellaneous:
  Cabin headroom: 4 feet, 4 inches.
  Portable potty fits under forward berth
  Foam flotation fore & aft
  Lightning grounded

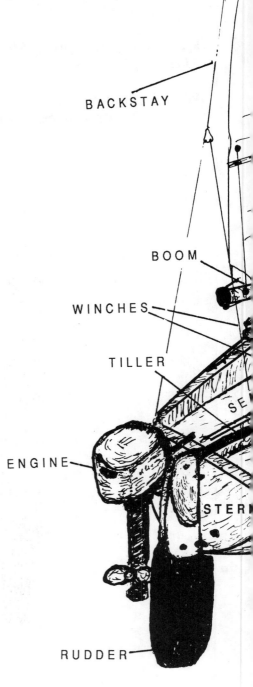

BACKSTAY

BOOM

WINCHES

TILLER

SE

ENGINE

STER

RUDDER

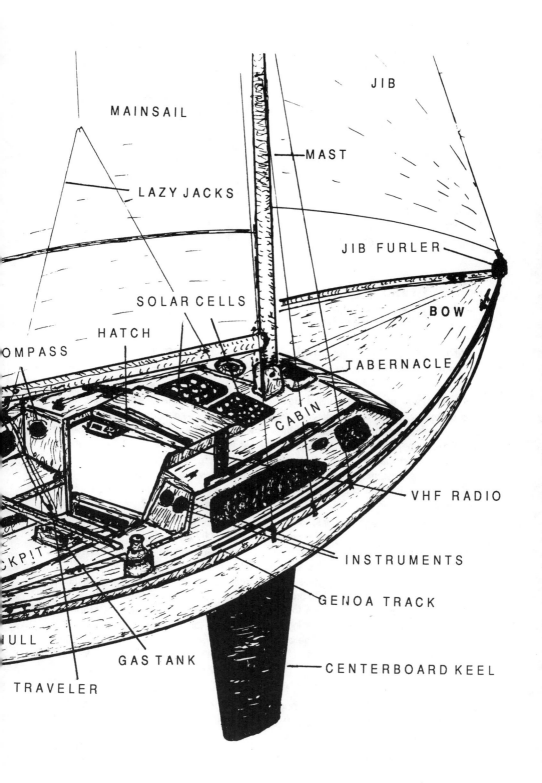

MAINSAIL

JIB

MAST

LAZY JACKS

JIB FURLER

SOLAR CELLS

BOW

HATCH

COMPASS

TABERNACLE

CABIN

VHF RADIO

INSTRUMENTS

GENOA TRACK

COCKPIT

HULL

GAS TANK

CENTERBOARD KEEL

TRAVELER

BOAT LOG & RECORD

IN THE TEETH OF THE NORTHEASTER

"The ultimate boat addict's Boat Book." — *Star-Tribune*, Minneapolis

"Fascinating."
— *Sail* magazine.

Every skipper ought to have the **Boat Log & Record** to keep track of voyages and to maintain a permanent record of the vessel and its needs. With its spiral binding and large, lay-flat pages, the **Boat Log & Record** is the best and most complete book of its kind. It makes boating more fun, safer, and trouble-free.

There are seven large sections, including equipment and maintenance record, purchasing organizer, and a commissioning checklist. The book simplifies boat management and maintenance chores and has instructions for heavy weather procedures and emergencies. Records up to 50 cruises. Lots more! **Note:** This is the log & record book designed by Marlin Bree and carried on board *Persistence* and *Tullamore Dew*. **Only $16.95**

For one summer, Marlin Bree sailed alone on Lake Superior in a 20-foot wooden sailboat he built in his backyard. His journey has been called *Blue Highways* by boat and likened to *Walk Across America*. In this best-seller, he writes about shipwrecks, storms, kind-hearted waterfront people, early voyageurs, gold, and an island of silver that was once the world's richest mine.

In the Teeth of the Northeaster has tales of seafaring on the world's largest freshwater lake (surface area), including the last hours of the *Edmund Fitzgerald*. Ultimately, Bree encountered a storm like those that make Superior one of the world's most dangerous bodies of water. "...will set your teeth on edge." — *Rocky Mountain News*. **Only $14.95**

You can buy these fine books at book or gift stores or order them directly from Marlor Press, 4304 Brigadoon Dr., St. Paul, MN 55126, or by calling toll free 800-669-4908. Visa and Master Card orders are accepted by telephone during business hours. Include $3 for shipping and handling.

INDEX

Marlin Bree, the author of *Call of the North Wind*, once lived along Lake Superior's shores and is an inveterate boater. He is also the author of *In the Teeth of the Northeaster: A Solo Voyage on Lake Superior,* and the *Boat Log and Record*. Bree co-authored the national best-seller, *Alone Against the Atlantic,* with sailor Gerry Spiess. Bree is an editorial contributor to *Northern Breezes* and *Sailing* magazines.